Bernard O'Reilly

Greenland, the Adjacent Seas, and the North-West Passage to the Pacific Ocean

During the Summer 1817 (1818)

weitsuechtig

Bernard O'Reilly

Greenland, the Adjacent Seas, and the North-West Passage to the Pacific Ocean

During the Summer 1817 (1818)

ISBN/EAN: 9783943850864

Auflage: 1

Erscheinungsjahr: 2013

Erscheinungsort: Bremen, Deutschland

weitsuechtig

GREENLAND,

THE

ADJACENT SEAS,

AND

THE NORTH-WEST PASSAGE

TO THE

PACIFIC OCEAN.

ILLUSTRATED IN A

VOYAGE TO DAVIS'S STRAIT,

During the Summer of 1817.

BY BERNARD O'REILLY, Esq.

NEW-YORK:

PUBLISHED BY JAMES EASTBURN AND CO
AT THE LITERARY ROOMS, BROADWA
Clayton & Kingsland, Printers,

....

1818.

CONTENTS.

INTRODUCTION.

ANCIENT HISTORY OF GREENLAND.

The history of northern nations is much involved in the mists of antiquity, which, like the fogs constantly met with in northern regions, are apt to magnify objects beheld through such a medium. The poems of Ossian owe their beautiful imagery to such delineation; the Icelandic Annals, detailing splendours highly apocryphal, may be looked upon as a venerable, but appropriate illustration of the same remark; and no portion of the globe, with regard to early times, affords more instances of such fondness for the sublime, than may be found in the History of Ireland.

Ancient Scandinavia also, on the weather-beaten and lichen-clad rock, presents many Runic carvings expressive of the fame of early heroes, who, in the admiration of their followers, became objects of deification. The ruins of an extensive city on the banks of the Irtish excited the curiosity of some travellers, and they there found vellum manuscripts stored up, which were watched with religious care by the barbarous inhabitants of the ruins. The travellers, however, contrived to possess themselves of a few of those records; and part, being sent to the French Academy, were deciphered as being some religious decrees written in an old Tartarian dialect in use about the age of Tamerlane, who, previously to his grand conquests in India, was nothing but a powerful northern lord. Modern Russia even owes to writers of polished talent, contemporary with the more improved state of that empire, rather than to the rude legends of her own inhabitants, whatever of elegance is flung over her early history.

With regard to the present subject, the scantiness of materials to form an interesting history of Greenland, renders the undertaking unsatisfactory and ungracious; but, with the reader's indulgence, so much shall be detailed as appears most consistent with fact. The particulars have been carefully selected from such authorities as are the most respectable on this head.

Snorro Sturleggen, who lived in the twelfth century, is stated to have been the author of the Speculum Regale, a compilation of ancient Icelandic rhymes, collected in the year 1215. This is the first historic light to guide inquiry in the history of Greenland. The next writer to be noticed is Torfæus, who was by birth an Icelander. His book bears the title of Grænlandia Antiqua. Torfæus appears to have employed Sturleggen's work as an inexhaustible source of fact, his whole context being little else than a transcript from that memorable legend. This writer dates the first discovery of Greenland by Europeans, in the year 982 of the Christian era; and on his authority is founded the early history of Greenland as connected with the European world.

With respect to the commentaries of Torfæus, much caution is adviseable in admitting his details, as the state of science in the times in which he wrote, and the great difficulties attending expeditions by sea in those rude ages, together with the exaggerations that such adventures would naturally give rise to, must perplex or mislead.

The writers of those times were possessed of a chivalrous spirit to exalt the character of their countrymen, and the very act of undertaking or effecting a voyage was sufficient to afford the adventuring hero a distinguished place in the historical record of the times.

The Danish Missionary Crantz has endeavoured to make up for the deficiencies of his predecessors in relating the history of Greenland. That writer used the materials of a primitive missionary, Egede, who published an account of his great and extraordinary endeavours to benefit the native Greenlanders. The difficulties Egede had to encounter, even in the outset of his undertaking, were excessive; but, in 1721, he at length succeeded in obtaining permission from the King of Denmark to proceed on his humane purpose of communicating the gospel tidings to the supposed lost settlers from Norway, who, in the stories of the day, were said to inhabit the eastern shores of Greenland, about the sixty-fourth degree of north latitude. Accordingly, in the same year, the worthy and pious missionary arrived at Baal's River, being driven thither, rather than succeeding in his endeavours to gain the point of coast to which the prevailing traditions of the time directed him. At the above place native Greenlanders were found, who expressed the greatest reluctance to any settlement being made upon their shores.

This account seems to have but little weight even with Crantz, the writer who repeats it. He possessed a strong imagination, involved in all the Bible commentaries of the day, and, though evidently possessed of much capacity of thought, appears not to have availed himself of the great and abundant materials for observation, which his situation afforded him, but was obliged to eke out a tardy volume of ecclesiastical detail to gratify his German patrons. The confusion of dates in Crantz's book is extremely perplexing, and is calculated very much to mislead inquiry.

The cold which prevails in the arctic regions is also another source of difficulty in the endeavour to procure accurate information regarding those countries from the natives, and the harsh medium of the Danish language, and uncertain transfer of intelligence through the Danish interpreter, renders an application to that intent generally fruitless, or at best unsatisfactory.

As to the poor Greenlanders, little information can be had from them regarding the history of their nation. They are said to have no "oral, nor written records;" but some traces of tradition are cherished among them to encourage the rising generation to imitate the exploits of some distinguished progenitor, who left a deathless fame by his skill and intrepidity in killing seals. Yet what can such tradition avail in the search for historic information? With regard to the Greenlander, such inquiry is unavailing; and their dislike of strangers intruding on their fishing haunts renders it equally useless to seek from them any accurate account of their present masters. On this point, the European historians remain the only resource.

The authors above referred to, namely Snorro Sturleggen, who is said to be the writer of the "Speculum Regale," and his commentator Torfæus, and latterly Egede and his commentator Crantz, appear to be the most distinguished amongst those who have written of Greenland. The accounts of those writers fix the discovery of that country in the year 982. But Claudius Christophersen, otherwise Lyscander, a divine, has conjectured the date of that event to be in the year 770. The latter rests on reference to a Bull of Pope Gregory IV. dated in the year 835, wherein the conversion of the Icelanders and Greenlanders is expressly committed to the first northern apostle, named Ansgarius.

These conjectures have much importance attached to them, as they lay the foundation of emigration from Europe at a very early period, however unfixed that period may be. The subsequent accounts refer generally to other migrations from the same quarter, having various objects in view: some to propagate the Gospel anew; others to retrace the steps pointed out by annals, at that time often copied in gilt character; others again, urged by the love of gain, to recover possession of such treasures as were reported to exist in those lands of wine, honey, corn, and cattle. These various pursuits were concentrated under one head, the finding of Old or Lost Greenland. How such an inquiry became necessary shall be next the subject of research.

It appears from the early accounts that Eric Raude, an enterprising chieftain, by birth a Norwegian, being compelled to go into banishment, was the first discoverer of Greenland. An expedition was fitted out the following year, consisting of twenty-five ships, fourteen of which only arrived. Where the point of destination lay, the story does not inform; yet wherever those adventurers landed they found such people as answer the description of the Greenlanders of the present day. Thorfin, an Icelandic chieftain, is said to have discovered Wineland, which is conjectured to be Newfoundland, where he also met with a similar people. They called them Skrællings, which means persons of a diminutive size, and which the reader will hereafter find is consonant to modern observation. The native Greenlanders have amongst them some confused and imperfect accounts of the Kablunæt, that is, the European, having called them by the name of Karalit, which, from their mode of omitting the first letter of words different from their own, bears a resemblance to Skrælling, and in some degree maintains the credit of the tradition.

One remarkable trait in the character of this people is an insurmountable aversion to the presence of intruders; and such they consider every one who is not of their own nation. In whatever manner they and the new-comers agreed, whether adopting their usual measure, of withdrawing to a remote distance to leave the helpless strangers to perish, or to retire from their fisheries, is not related. Ivar Beer, an early historian, mentions, that Greenland was inhabited and tilled both on the eastern and western sides, in the fourteenth century. This is further confirmed by another statement, which represents Lief, the son of Eric Raude, coming to Norway, in 999, to report on the state of Greenland. Adam Bremensis, who wrote in the eleventh century, makes mention of Lief having discovered Newfoundland, in the year 1001, and went the year following to Greenland, probably on his father's course, and met with Skrællings in boats.

Accounts thus far considered may, in a great degree, establish the fact of the Norwegians and Icelanders having been the first Europeans who can claim the discovery of Greenland. Yet it must be admitted, that others had the merit of discovering it before them; for the former visiters found a people of small stature already in possession. The Norwegian relations go no higher than the sixty-fourth degree, which is about the entrance to Baal's River on the west side, and the promontory of Herjolf's Ness, in the sixty-third degree on the eastern side. The former was the principal place of the colony; and between these two points were situate numerous little settlements, at present said to be indicated by their ruins, the largest of which are visible on the south-eastern extremity of the country between Staten Hook and Frobisher's Straits. These ruins, of churches and large dwellings, are a further support to the foregoing statement; but the natives about Baal's River, when asked for the explanation of the name of a particular place there, describe it as the place where men shot arrows at one another. Here then it appears the extirpation of the Europeans began, which was carried round the settlements in savage fury by the Skrællings, until the country became their own again; or, if any survived the massacre, cold, privations, and despair, must have effected their destruction.

In the fourteenth century, the Skrællings suddenly made their appearance in great numbers in West Greenland; and their first onset produced the death of eighteen Norwegians. This petty war continued long enough to obtai nfor the country the name of Old or Lost Greenland among Europeans; and the natives still remember the war of extermination carried on by their forefathers with the Kablunæt, that is, the European intruders, and their having bravely killed or expelled the invaders.

To another cause may also be attributed this catastrophe. In the year 1350, a great plague desolated nearly all Europe, but ravaged most severely the northern countries. Possibly the ruinous effects of this pestilence may have reached Greenland, and destroyed the scanty colonies there. Excessive cold is known to approximate, in its effects, to excessive heat; and to this cause principally is attributed the numerous and civilized population of Iceland having been swept away during a similar visitation. The journal of Bishop Egede records a similar waste of human life, among the natives, which he witnessed to be produced by the baneful contagion of the small-pox, introduced by the crews of some ships that conveyed thither a Moravian mission, in the year 1733, and which raged from September in that year, till the June following. At one place alone, 200 families of Greenlanders were cut off, leaving only eighteen survivors.

That the period of the former pestilence must have been singularly calamitous, is evident from the disappearance of an extensive island in the northern Atlantic, peopled with polished inhabitants dwelling in a hundred towns, which, shortly after its discovery, was suddenly overwhelmed in the ocean, and disappeared with every living creature on its surface.

About that time, the spirit of discovery was much indulged, and almost every country produced ardent adventurers. The people of Britain and Ireland were not inactive in this respect; the latter being represented as trading to West Friesland, the island abovementioned, for the sake of the fisheries. As no existing history of Ireland makes mention of this circumstance, the doubt may be lessened by stating, that it was part of the policy of Queen Elizabeth to deprive that island of her records, by which probably more mischief was done to the great cause of history than could be balanced by the little triumph of humbling a nation's pride.

Columbus, in entering on his immortal pursuit, came to Britain to carry his purpose by kingly assistance. He was refused the protection he sought; and Spain profited by his disappointment. Two noble Venetians following his example, obtained a ship in Ireland, and sailed to West Friesland, which their surprise at finding populous and flourishing caused them to announce as having been by them first discovered. The names of these Venetians are Nicholas and Anthony Zeni: their discovery is dated 1380. This island, West Friesland, was laid down in the fifty-eighth degree, between Iceland and Greenland. It is said to have been touched at by Frobisher, in one of his voyages in search of gold in Greenland. This spot is now marked on the charts as occupying an extensive and dangerous tract of ocean, and is named the Sunken Land of Buss. Mariners are studiously careful to avoid it. It is in tempestuous weather covered by a high and terrible sea. When humane reflection comes to contemplate this awful event, considerations of the most painful description must arise.

The darkness in which the northern history involves the fate of this island is peculiarly uninviting to accurate research. That there has been a West Friesland is by no means doubtful; and that such a country was not the Greenland of late note, is equally certain. The population in the hundred towns of this island, placed so far north as represented, and so far to the southward of Iceland, was well worthy of the notice of the historians of the time. The mind, however rude, in viewing the waves that still tower over its waste, must sicken at the contemplation. The site can only come within the casual glance of the wary mariner; and in the latitude of the Sunken Land such a man is guided by his fears to avoid the dangerous spot. Valleys of dreadful soundings, and peaks of tremendous and destructive contact, buried in the ocean water, forbid an exact inquiry regarding its actual position. That the island in question has been there, about the time mentioned, facts forbid us to disbelieve; whilst its fearful disappearance very naturally prevents the rarely passing stranger from exploring the actual depths thereabouts, in order to determine the dangerous circumstances of the ground.

Quære? May not this land of Buss so sunken bear some probable reference to the Old or Lost Greenland, or the Atalantis of the Greek writers? It would not be easy to disprove this.

It certainly must appear matter of surprise, that the name of these countries should still be Greenland, though even in less or more degree the peculiar scene of snow and ice. The accounts, on which popular belief has hitherto rested, inform the public by making a comparison between those regions and the island of Iceland, whence the early navigators sailed westward. Strange, that at a time when some imaginary hero, worthy of Runic record, some such man as Flokko is reported to have been, did not direct his followers to a place of such natural importance as West Friesland must have been, so contiguous, and so much towards the genial south. We must conclude, that the island so designated, the Atalantis of the Greeks, or the famed Ultima Thule, should have stood in more note than to escape the observation of men sailing for strange and consequently unknown countries. The name Greenland would in that event, that is, the discovery and colonization of a fine and fertile soil, afterwards studded with a hundred towns, have been more appropriately and significantly applied than to the barren peaks about Staten Hook, or Cape Farewell, or such other parts of southern Greenland, as must naturally present themselves first over the horizon to the eye of the voyager.

From the pen of one of the writers on this subject, we are told that the name Greenland was given to the countries where the Norwegians ventured to fix their settlements, in contradistinction to the bleak and snow-clad mountains of Iceland. Both, however, have been misapplied. If the early annals of Iceland be correct, the appellation of that island is derived from the immense quantities of ice annually driven on its shores; but no season of the year presents the aspect of Greenland (with the exception of rocky faces of mountains fronting a southern sun) without the presence of a cloak of snow, or a chilling curtain of ice. It is true, the elevated lands in Greenland produce in themselves such an absorption of solar heat, during the summer months, as to make the atmosphere insupportably sultry at certain hours, and during particular winds; but vegetation has not there sufficient life to warrant the use of such an application of the epithet green, as characterizing the general aspect of the country.

In examining into this part of the subject, recourse must be had to other means of elucidation than such conjecture, and, in the language of the natives, a criterion is discoverable. This harmless race have an expression for the sun which bears but little resemblance to any term in language hitherto regarded. Succanuk is their term for the luminary that brings them back their fishing months with his presence. In this his retirement southwards, the northern people say, "Succanuk is gone to Succanunga:" by this they describe all the lands where their fisheries are successful. Now through what source a synonyme for Succanunga may be traced to the language of nations very remote from this truly original people may appear matter of interesting speculation.

A classical reader, familiar with the works of Greek and Roman writers, will recollect that an epithet for the noonday Apollo, when clad in Latin form, is Grynæus. Grynæus Apollo forms an adulatory invocation in the prayer of Eneas, who was at once a priest and prince according to the Phrygian mythological system. General Vallancy, who bestowed much and very extraordinary labour on the subject of antiquities, particularly those referable to eastern origin, has fixed on the word Grian, of Irish or Celtic signification, as it may be received, being epithetically expressive of the strongest power of the sun, which is synonymous among all ancient nations with the Apollo of Grecian mythology. To avoid, therefore, invidious reference as to intercourse with the Greenlanders, it may be fairly admitted, that the synonyme, by whatever voyager to these parts communicated, is justly explained by the above terms: let us view them in connexion:

Succanuk—the Sun.	Succanunga—Greenland.
Grian—Apollo, or the Sun.	Grianland—Land of the Sun.

The Land of the Sun, or Sunny-land, as familiarly may be said, corresponds with the simple appellation which the natives give their country. The adventurers who came in aftertimes to seek the same shores, not probably understanding the meaning of the term, yet spelling the word as they could from hearing it often repeated, were inclined to write Grianland in their mode Groenland, which sounds very nearly alike, but in the language of Denmark has no reference to the original, and hence the absurdity of the application of such a name as Greenland to countries comparatively destitute of every product of nature that gives a green luxuriance and vegetative beauty to more southern climates.

The brief view of the subject thus laid down will suffice for such as are desirous to examine the more immediate purpose of this work. Histories of almost every explored portion of the globe crowd the shelves of libraries, and are at the hand of the hourly reader. The man, however, who scans human nature, who studies his connexion with the correlevant parts of creation, and who weighs his destinies, his responsibilities, his value in the great scale of being, will not be content with words alone, how plausibly soever authenticated. A wish to witness the facts as grounded on observation, denies him quiet, until doubt can be excluded by experience. He tries, travels, studies, deeply reflects, makes up his mind, and passes judgment. Such a rule should be the guide of any one intruding on public opinion. It is the same principle that exalts the British jurisprudence above that of every people on earth, in the heaven-born system of the trial by jury. Every honest man so seated is an Alfred, as each individual there forms his own opinion.

Such reflections actuated the mind of the writer of the following sheets previous to his undertaking. The object of inquiry appeared highly important. It seemed also involved in much mystery; and its development was viewed as matter of meritorious pursuit. A voyage to Davis's Straits was therefore undertaken for the purpose of obtaining satisfactory information on many points of natural history, hitherto untouched, or which had not been sufficiently elucidated. The circumstances of the voyage were of such a nature as left more for observation than a progress of discovery should be accompanied with. The reader, however, may rest assured that what shall be submitted to perusal is accurate, and such as many, enjoying the indulgences of warmer regions, would feel little inclination to witness.

CHAPTER I.

THE VOYAGE OUTWARD.

ON Saturday, March 8th, in the Thomas, of Hull, Wm. Brass, master, we left the roadstead at the Hawk in the River Humber, and at 9 a. m. cleared the Spurn lights. In the evening, the breeze becoming fresh at W. N. W. we tacked and stood round Flamborough Head into Burlington Bay. The breeze increasing to strong, we tacked again from Burlington Bay, and steered for the Orkneys, in a full breeze from W.

Before I proceed to the detail of matters contained in my journal, it is necessary to premise a few remarks, in order to make the contents of that record intelligible to every reader. In the course of a voyage, the direction of the winds, and their velocities, are of primary importance to be understood; and the signs by which their change, or expected commencement can be known, form one of the main objects in the experience of a seaman. The question of "How are we to have the wind?" is seldom addressed to a person not long accustomed to the sea. The aged coasting sailor prides himself as much upon knowing the influence of every point of land, with regard to the wind, as he does upon his knowledge of the set of tide: whilst the mariner, conversant with seas and oceans, where he has seldom any land to guide his observations, must look to the general indication of the sky and clouds for sure information. I have frequently observed that an old seaman, on turning out for his watch, invariably directs his attention to see how the sky looks: next, turning to the compass, he silently observes the direction of the wind. During his silence one may, on such occasions, evidently notice the operation of his mind drawing conclusions from such observations. Hence appeared the importance of making a few remarks on these matters; and as I am not aware that any thing has yet been said conclusively on the subject, I shall indulge the presumption that there is some degree of novelty in what I am about to state.

The great principle of electricity is now generally considered as the cause of both clouds and winds; for to these two subjects I am inclined to confine its operation, though undoubtedly it discharges a most active agency throughout creation. In a dry atmosphere it seems to be in greatest energy, though less observably in action. In the formation and destruction or decomposition of clouds, it is more visible in its effects; but in the direction of the winds, it possesses a sovereign power of impulse. The presence of electricity in dry air is manifest in experiments, wherein all moisture must be carefully removed, else this celestial agent does not appear. The immortal Franklin detected its presence in the clouds, and forced it to descend, from that species or rather genus of cloud, nimbus, in which it is usually concentrated; and its presence, when in motion, is familiar to every one experimenting with an electrical machine, when, as the cylinder is revolved, a wind is sensibly felt if the hand is placed near the cylinder. The presence of this principle in the clouds is very remarkable during the formation of the cloud above mentioned, being what is familiarly called the thunder cloud.

Mr. Howard has lately laid down a classification of the clouds, by which this branch of natural history has been signally simplified. The reader is requested to refer to that ingenious gentleman's publication. His theory has been also copied at length into Mr. Forster's book on Clouds,* wherein many curious illustrations of this subject are inserted. As my applications were on a scale of more than 3,000 miles in extent, with a perfectly natural horizon almost perpetually under observation, I trust that the details, which shall be as brief as possible, will not be subjected to a charge of presumption on the patience of the reader. I may be also pardoned the expression of my own feeling of their importance to the great concerns of navigation and trade. And as, in consequence of such views of nature, on general principles, as I hope to exhibit in the progress of this work, the great Atlantic and Northern seas in general may, ere long, become the theatre of more frequent commerce, other benefits may be found to arise from the conclusions to be drawn from these observations.

With regard then to clouds, I shall take the classical names laid down by Mr. Howard; and leaving the discussion of his elegant theory in abler hands,

* Researches about Atmospheric Phenomena, by Thomas Forster, F. L. S.

must beg that gentleman's indulgence, in placing them in such arrangement as I found, from experience, to be most useful in application. To this classification, a concise exposition shall be added, by way of illustration, for such readers as may not have seen Mr. Howard's exposition. This illustration is intended merely to convey a clear idea of the colour and general situation of the clouds. Therefore, beginning with the lowest member of the classification, we shall proceed with the next in simplicity, and then to their various compounds, pointing out the probable agency of each. Taking nubes then for the term expressive of the genus, the names of the species are as follow:

Genus.	Species.	
Nubes.	Stratus......	Lowest of all clouds. Evening and morning ground mist.
———	Cirrus......	Highest ditto. Mares' Tails. Mackarel sky, &c.
———	Cumulus......	Small dense cloud, increasing upwards, base horizontal.
———	Cirrostratus....	The common loose vapoury cloud, generally of a brownish colour. In profile, it represents the figure of a fish; sometimes a dark streak, and lying parallel to the horizon; sometimes descending very dark at a sharp or acute angle. It is the most variable of all clouds, and is usually intermediate between the others.
———	Cirrocumulus..	Next in height to cirrus, generally white, in round, irregular, or diamond patches, or representing small waves; the last form usually precedes a high wind.

Genus.	Species.	
Nubes.	Cumulostratus..	The previous form of nimbus, called by seamen the "land cloud," being at a distance like rocks and mountains, having, according to its position with the sun, round and rugged snowy tops, dark body, base of the same or deep-bluish black, horizontal and ragged, or cirrose; moves often against the wind.*
——	Nimbus........	The cumulostratus discharging rain, hail, lightning, &c.

Having thus briefly enumerated the different species of clouds, a few observations on their most obvious uses may not be out of place. The cirrus, ascending, assumes some modification of cirrostratus; and owing to some principles, probably communicated from its auxiliary, the latter puts on such a variety of colours as it generally presents. The rainbow, and also many other luminous phenomena, appear in this medium. Cirrostratus is the store from which the cumulus is collected; whilst the latter becomes by agglomeration the cumulostratus. The cumulostratus, being charged with the electric fluid, changes to nimbus, which subsequently becomes cirrostratus again. Cirrostratus, when elevated to a higher and drier atmosphere, is changed into the form of cirrocumulus, in which the electric principle seems to be less active than in the others. This beautiful cloud is the ornament of summer and tranquil skies, and is by the simple pen of Bloomfield described as having

"the beauteous semblance of a flock at rest."

* "Noctem hiememque ferens."

When the electric fluid is called into action, this cloud, viz. the cirrocumulus, if not previously dissolved in the surrounding atmosphere, undergoes a rapid change. Shortly after, the long, fine flaxen cirrus, exhibits its slender forms, sometimes in a single silvery line; sometimes like the fabled tresses of Ariadne; at other times, when crossed by an ascending or descending current of electricity, it exhibits an elegant representation of waves. Previous to a storm, its changes are most rapid, and its form often evanescent. At all times, it is considered the index of the electric fluid; and one accustomed to its direction can venture to predict, with tolerable certainty, the approach and degree of force of a wind, many hours, nay, often days, before the change takes place. To seafaring people, a knowledge of the forms and situation of this cloud is essential to security.

The next object to which I shall invite the reader's attention, is an enumeration of winds, and such principally as are most familiar to the navigator of the Atlantic ocean. In order to render this subject more easily understood, I shall present the names of the several winds in Latin, sheltering the attempt under respectable authority. They shall however be accompanied with the familiar synonymes in use among nautical men.

The ancients denominated the winds known to them, not according to their force, which should naturally indicate a proper classification, but with reference to some local circumstance, such as blowing from a distant country, or some of the cardinal points. The present arrangement applies to the relative forces of the several winds, by which means it becomes easy of universal application.

I propose therefore to enumerate seven genera; the first five, with their species, being arranged with respect to their several velocities; the last two, with a reference to their peculiar effects. As to the accuracy of the Latin names, I may presume that it rests on classic ground. Ovid, in the tragic tale of Procris, has given authority for using the term expressive of the first genus; and the prince of Latin verse has, with the exception of the last, sanctioned all the rest by his adoption.

Dr. Franklin has, in his peculiar grandeur of simple observation, noted the progress of hurricane to be at the rate of 100 miles per hour. On this plain scale, the comparative velocities of the other winds are calculated (reference being specially had, wherever their forces could be ascertained, with regard to the motion of a ship's way) under their influence, severally. It is matter of regret that circumstances did not allow me to check this calculation by an anemometer.

Subjoined to the foregoing is a table giving a view of a ship, according to her trim or canvass, in each wind, and her knots under the influence of each. This chiefly refers to a whale ship, but may be applicable to other vessels. The table includes the effects of wind favourable, or the contrary.

WINDS.

Nautical Names.		Rate of Knots per Hour.	Latin Names.		Velocity per Hour.
Gen.	Spec.		Gen.	Spec.	
Air,	Light,	2	Aura,	Spirans,	5 miles
Breeze,	Light,	4	Zephyrus,	Lenis,	10 ditto
———	Fresh,	7 to 8	———	Felix,	15 ditto
———	Strong,	9	———	Agens,	20 ditto
Gale,	Fresh,	10 and more	Ventus,	Celer,	25 ditto
——	Strong,	10 and much more	———	Rapidus,	35 ditto
——	Hard,	10 to 12 and more	———	Vehemens,	45 ditto
Tempest,		Unknown	Tempestas,	Ruens,	75 ditto
Hurricane,		Ditto	Hiems,	Rapiens,	100 ditto
Whirlwind,		Ditto	Procella,	Gyrans,	Unknown
Simoom,		Ditto	Simooma,	Suffocans.	Ditto

WINDS.

	State of Ships in a fair Wind.		State of Ships in a contrary Wind.	
Names of Winds.	Rate.	Canvass carried.	Rate.	Canvass carried.
Light air	2 knots	Full sail	2 knots	All sails set
Light breeze	4	Full sail	3	All sails set
Strong breeze	7 to 8	Full sail	4 to 5	All sails set
Strong breeze	9	Full sail	6 to 7	All sails set
Fresh gale	10	Full sail	6 to 7	Top-gal. sails furled
Strong gale	10+	Reefed topsails Top-gallant sails full	5 to 4	Close-reef'd topsails
Hard gale	10+	Close-reefed topsails and reefed courses	3	Close reef'd main-top-sail, and reef'd fore-sail
Tempest	1½ drift	Ship laid to, under close-reefed main-topsail	1½ drift	Ship laid to as before. Tops struck
Hurricane	Unknown	Ship drifting under bare poles.	Unknown	Same as in fair wind

Having premised so much, in the hope that the matter will not be deemed irrelevant to the main object of the observations, which is the professed aim of the work, particularly as they will aid in elucidating many of the atmospheric phenomena hereinafter to be mentioned, I shall proceed very briefly indeed with the Journal. But first in the following short space shall say a word or two about the Orkney Islands.

The general appearance of those islands is that of low, flat, rounded hills, with the exception of the western side of Hoy and Pomona, which present a bold rocky front of sand-stone to the ocean. The stratification seldom departs from horizontally; in many places consisting of large flags lying loosely over each other. The soil is poor, and yields little corn; the inhabitants subsisting chiefly on fish. Latterly the straw plait manufacture being introduced, employs the younger girls: this is chiefly at Stromness, which is the usual rendezvous of ships proceeding to the westward, or to the fisheries. Kirkwall, the chief town, is respectable, and is remarkable for its fine cathedral. Though scarcely a shrub is to be seen on Pomona; it is said to have been once well wooded, and trunks of large trees are often dug up.

On the 17th of April,* after being about six weeks at sea, on making a tack towards land, I had a distinct

* JOURNAL.

Thursday, March 13: thermometer 42°, 43°, 42°: wind W. S. W., strong breeze: under shelter of Duncansbay Head: a detached high rock of red-brown sandstone, about 100 yards from the shore, is called Johnny Groat's Castle: this day clear and dry: squalls eddying along the sea.

March 14: ther. 46°, 47°, 40°: wind N. W., almost a calm: sky clear and delightfully serene: Stromness in sight.

March 15: ther. 41°, 44°, 42°: wind S., light breeze: cir-

view of West Greenland. A most dreary appearance characterizes this part of that country. Some small islands lay along the coast, between which were imbedded bergs of out-topping height, and in their peaks and prominences mimicking the forms of land. In the intervals of snow, the dark

rus changing into cirrocumulus, cirrostratus: weather fine: anchored at the back of the Holms, a flat island, at Stromness.

March 16: ther. 46°, 45°, 40°: wind S. S. W., light breeze: cirrostratus in long dark beds in the westward, tinged red with the rays of the setting sun.

March 17: ther. 42°, 45°, 40°: wind W., fresh breeze: stratus all around, probably from the ocean spray, cirrostratus radiating from the S. W.

March 18: ther. 47°, 45°, 40°: wind S. W. fresh breeze: scud at a great elevation. The wind of this day had been indicated by the cirrostratus radiation of the preceding: the reader is requested to bear this circumstance in recollection: partial cirrocumulus.

March 19: ther. 34°, 25°, 30°: wind W. S. W., strong breeze: cirrostratus drifting with sleet and snow in the evening.

March 20: ther. 24°, 30°, 25°: wind N. N. E., hard gale: nimbus discharging large hail and snow. The thermometer, after the first observation, rose to 30°, and on the approach of the nimbus, suddenly fell to 25°, and there remained.

March 21: ther. 27°, 46°, 26°: wind N. E., light breeze: cirrostratus: cumulus: nimbus occupying half the welkin in N. W. and discharging hail: land covered with snow: weather became unusually fine: during the night an excellent exhibition of cirrus traversing the sky, pointing from E. and S. E. towards W. and N. W.: this evening put to sea.

March 22: ther. 34°, 36°, 33°: wind S. W. by W., light breeze: scud, drifting from N. E.: wind increased to strong breeze: a strong swell of the ocean from W. N. W.

rock put forth its wrinkled brow, the dip of fissure appearing about fifteen degrees. The mountains in the distance exhibited high sharp peaks, and to the eye of a stranger they appear the most dismal and chilling sight in nature. This land is north of Joris Bay, and is seldom seen.

March 23: ther. 36° throughout: wind W. N. W., strong breeze: wind of this day was indicated by the cirrus of the 21st: various bodies of cirrostratus, discharging sleet and hail at times: sea continues running very high from the W. N. W.

March 24: ther. 36°, 34°, 28°: wind W. N. W., hard gale: broken nimbus, discharging snow and sleet with great violence: sea very high: numerous gulls seen: observed the larus canus, marinus, fuscus, in great numbers, also ridibundus and cataractes: towards evening more moderate: sky milky blue.

March 25: ther. 38°, 35°, 30°: wind N. W., fresh breeze: cirrostratus overcast: showers of evanescent snow: moon appearing in a double halo; the inner circle deep yellow; the outer, with the iris rings, very distinct.

March 26: ther. 34°, 36°, 35°: wind N. by E., strong breeze: weather fine: cumulostratus and cumulus near the horizon: an immense pile of cumulostratus occupying all the W. and S. W. region: afternoon, a sudden and violent gale blew from that quarter during three hours, attended with sleet: procellaria glacialis.

At half past nine p. m., the polar coruscation (aurora borealis) was very vivid; the crown forming a portion of a circle in the zenith, curving from N. W. to S. E.; the brightest emanation running to the southward, then traversing sideways, with fairy speed, in conical spires from E. N. E. to W. S. W. on an invisible base, nearly parallel with the horizon, but descending from the north.

The moon, at the same time, shown faintly through a corona in intervening diffuse cirrostratus, around which was an extensive halo. Mr. Forster states the halo as ordinarily about 45° in ra-

On the 28th of April, three natives, the first I had yet seen, came up with the ship, and being lifted into a boat, canoes and all, they came aboard, and bartered some parts of their dress with the men. After a stay of three hours they departed. They came from some low islands north of Baal's River.

dius: by that proportion the halo here observed must have been more than twice that extent of radius. The luminous ring here noticed exhibited none of the iridescent colours, but was of a sickly yellowish white; the area scarcely differing from the exterior, except that portion in which the corona appeared.

This phenomenon having attracted my attention, I remained on deck till midnight, and conversing with an experienced seaman on the subject, I learned that such appearances in this latitude generally preceded very high wind. The increasing temperature, noted this day, was a further indication of an approaching wind from the southward.

There was a dead calm immediately after the coruscation disappeared: the atmosphere very clear.

March 27: ther. 42°, 46°, 43°: Wind S. by W., strong breeze: sky overcast with dense, diffuse cirrostratus: sun in Corona: wind increased to strong gale:* procellaria glacialis.

March 28: ther. 38°, 43°, 36°: wind S. by W., fresh breeze: nimbus with snow: cumulostratus in masses.

March 29: ther. 38°, 38°, 36°: wind N. W., strong breeze: sky generally clear: cumulostratus changing into nimbus, with mixed showers of hail, rain, and snow: atmosphere unusually cold to sensation, even at the degree marked by the thermometer: ship steering to S. W.: a large balæna physalus (finner) passed the ship. Larus canus: at 8 p. m., the electric coruscations suddenly appeared, running at about thirty degrees above

* This event proves the observations of the 26th to be correct.

Their lower extremities were remarkably small. They strike an object at twenty yards distance with surprising dexterity. The figure of one, when seated in his canoe, almost compels the imagination to look upon the man and his boat as partaking of a common existence, restoring to some de-

the horizon, ascending in a perpendicular direction from a base in a rapid succession of brassy yellow flames from W. to E. and soon died away.

Immediately after, from the westward there slowly extended upwards to the zenith four faintly marked radii, which diverged as they ascended; two, more approximating to each other and nearly of equal breadth throughout. One only remained, stretching in a magnificent arch over the zenith, embracing the horizon E. and W., and of a splendour exceedingly faint: it might, on hasty observation, be supposed a cirrus. The reader is requested to bear this in mind, as it will be necessary to refer to this phenomenon hereafter.

March 30: ther. 35°, 36°, 35°: wind N. W., fresh breeze, increasing to a gale: cumulostratus, successively advancing with the wind, becoming nimbus in its angry progress, and regularly discharging hail with intensity of cold. In this immense basin (the Atlantic) the effects of wind this day have been commensurate to the grandest elevation of wave. The firmness of the vessel giving all the security of land observation, I looked on this terrible scene with awful delight. At 9¼ p. m. the coruscations appeared again from N. W.; and in the midst of the stunning hurly, I could not resist noticing their activity. Imagination would say, that truly the spirit of the storm was abroad in all his majesty. The account of the lights, immediately noted, may be of interest to some of my readers.

Assuming, as before, an archwise coruscation, but instead of the illucescent radii playing from a horizontal base as formerly observed, the basial line of these coruscations assumed an angle from the horizon of about fifty degrees. Tongues of brassy hue,

gree of reality the fable of the Centaur; particularly when these poor people are seen flying along, each in his flimsy bark, with a short paddle alternately pressed along the thing in which he securely sits, regardless of wave or wind. The jacket they wear is lashed so as to prevent the admission of water,

at considerable intervals of space, and bending to S. W., touched their ethereal base with lambent playfulness, then, twining in spiral convolution, shot rapidly upwards, and spent themselves in the more elevated regions of the atmosphere.

March 31 : ther. 42°, 44°, 40° : wind S. by W., strong gale : scud flying furiously along: in the course of this day the weather has been highly variable, and sometimes rain : the change of wind was pre-indicated by the aurora of the preceding.

April 1 : ther. 33° throughout : wind W. N. W., hard gale : sky uniformly overcast with cirrostratus : the gale increasing in fury, the sea rose literally mountain high : procellaria glacialis : moon in halo of vivid brightness.

April 2 : ther. 34°, 35°, 36° : wind W. N. W., hard gale : storm unabated : cloud beginning to break : procellaria glacialis.

April 3 : ther. 42°, 44°, 40° : wind S.W., strong gale : overcast cirrostratus : less dense; long, dark beds of the same, sometimes seen through, moving slowly from S. E. : sun very dimly seen in corona : some rain fell : sea higher, if possible, than yesterday : the zenith clearing a little in the afternoon, admitted a view of linear, comoid, and undulate cirrus, pointing south of east : cloud becoming cumulescent.*

* This night, as the clouds of the cirrocumulus form drifted along, a similar radiation to that noticed in Journal 29th ult. occurred. A stream of the electric fluid, coming from S. E., dissolved the cirrocumulus in its progress, and left it behind as a splendid white arch extending across the sky. The cirrus of this afternoon visibly pointed towards the quarter whence the radiation subsequently came.

whilst all is snug within. Their fishing tackle and darts are so placed as to be constantly within reach, and safe from accident, by a simple fastening of thongs. Every thing was exceedingly neat: their outer dress is water proof.

The appearance of the land to the southward of

April 4: ther. 42°, 34°, 32°: wind W. S. W., fresh gale: the storm begins to abate: sky generally clear: cirrus and nimbus: larus canus, marinus, tridactylus, and procellaria glacialis.

April 5: ther. 42°, 44°, 41°: wind W. N. W., fresh breeze: sky overcast: atmosphere mild: a meteor descended to the S. W. (it generally moves towards an expected wind): it was of small magnitude, and visible for about a second.

April 6: ther. 46°, 45°, 44°: wind S. W., fresh gale: overcast cirrostratus, with some rain, at times very heavy: wind abating, the sea became more tranquil, nearly altogether so: slight appearance of coruscation in W. N. W.: it is remarked that in high northern latitudes they indicate a northerly wind.

April 7: 36°, 33°, 34°: wind W. N. W., fresh breeze increasing: towards evening a cumulostratus began to form in N.; and, as it became an intensely dark nimbus, it advanced from that point with an unusual brightness in its rear and above. This brightness is considered a sign of wind from the point where it appears: polar lights vivid: a trainless meteor passed S. W.

April 8: ther. 37°, 43°, 41°: wind N., light breeze: weather fine: cirrostratus in deep brown beds; had a settled appearance, and died away without changing position: lights very vivid, restless, and playing from every point towards the star Benetnach, as to a centre of afflux.

April 9: ther. 41°, 44°, 41°: wind W. N. W. to W. S. W., light breeze: sky overcast with light misty rain: drops scarcely discernible.

April 10: ther. 42°, 48°, 43°: wind S. W., strong breeze: thick, damp, hazy weather, at times sultry, clearing towards evening: procellaria glacialis numerous, and larus canus.

Cape Monkchese and about Queen Anne's Cape, which was seen by us on the 1st of May, is generally that of uniform, sharp, angular eminences. Nothing but barren rock constitutes this coast, rising in successive peaks, not much elevated above the horizon. Being at times distant not more than twelve miles, the

April 11 : ther. 43°, 48° 40° : wind S. W., fresh breeze : cirrostratus generally diffused, with heavy rain.

April 12 : ther. 35°, 40°, 38° : wind W., fresh breeze : atmosphere dry and clear : scattered patches of cirrostratus : heavy pieces of ice (fragments of bergs) drifting past ; sailing by a pack of ice : fine cirrus pointing from N. E.

April 13 : ther. 36°, 38°, 34° : wind W. S. W., fresh gale : steering S. by W. ½ W. to avoid the ice : the pack seems to be a limited and solitary one, as the ice blink (a peculiar brightness in the horizon) is no longer discernible : some parallel beds of cirrostratus in profile : all else clear : high land appearing above the horizon, supposed to be Staten Hook or Cape Farewell : procellaria gulosa, and a species of mergus too distant to be recognised in view : a pair of fringilla tristis alighted on the ship, and afterwards flew towards east ; in the evening passed a stream of ice : passed a large berg over whose lower extremity the sea broke, as upon a rock : two seals seen.

April 14 : ther. 30°, 35°, 30° : wind N. W., strong breeze : light brown patches of cirrostratus : cleared the pack : detached cumulus apparently motionless : the heavy manner in which the procellaria glacialis plies his wing would indicate a southerly wind (at 5 p. m. the atmosphere has just undergone a very remarkable change, proving its direct influence on the animal system : sky dully bright : light flaky snow : wind nearly calm) : polar lights very vivid, running from E. and points S. of east.

April 15 : ther. 38°, 40°, 35° : wind S. b. W., light breeze : weather very fine : procellaria glacialis, larus maximus, a flock of L. tridactylus : the weather gall * seen in S. E.

* A remarkable cloud of singular hue, being of a deep indigo blue, with a dash ..ow, which gives it a greenish cast. It generally appears embosomed in

observer has them distinctly enough in view, particularly with the aid of a good telescope. Very rarely did any rounded summit appear, and the extremely few in number of that description were nearest to the shore, and showed the characteristic sharp fracture of basalt. Some huts were also discernible. No ap-

April 16 : ther. 30° throughout : wind S. E., strong gale : cirrostratus overcast : snow and sleet : sea streaked with foam : the lights, between 10 and 11 p. m. were exceedingly splendid, and seemed to make Benetnach a centre, but moving to N. E.

April 17 : ther. 28° throughout : wind N. W., fresh breeze : light vapoury cirrostratus : the presence of cumulostratus to S. E. indicates land seen four to two leagues distant : this being dangerous, stood out to sea : procellaria glacialis, larus maximus, balæna rostrata.

April 18 : ther. 28°, 26°, 25° : wind E. S. E., strong breeze increasing : the whole of this day slightly overcast, and light hard snow falling : circle of view not more than half a mile in radius : P. glacialis * on wing, going directly north : L. maximus and mate.

April 19 : ther. 21°, 19°, 15° : wind E. N. E., hard gale : sea very high : sky still overcast with snow cloud : the ropes and sails covered with ice : cold intense to sensation : snow falls sharp and of icy form, transparent : P. glacialis unusually active : one L. maximus seen.

April 20 : ther. 10°, 8½°, 11°, 9° : wind N. N. E. to N. N. W., fresh gale, varying every instant, abated to fresh breeze : sky overcast continually with snow cloud : the ocean spray, as it rises, congealed into icy mist : no effect of freezing on nitrous, muriatic, or sulphuric acid, or on rum : the heats of atmosphere this day extraordinary at intervals during the gale.

other clouds, occupying a very small space. This weather gall is dreaded by seamen, as a severe wind generally comes from the place where it appears. For distinction sake, I beg to refer to the colour of this cloud for the expression "stormy blue."

* The P. glacialis is a sure guide to the whale hunters.

pearance of a plain, not even an inch, presented itself in an extent of coast of more than fifty miles this day; and as far as the sight could ascertain from the highest point of observation, the land inward seemed to be uniformly of the same conformation, but the mountains appeared much higher. From the depth of snow

April 21: ther. 10°, 12°, 9°, 11°: wind N. by E., light breeze, westing towards evening, and nearly calm: cirrostratus illuminated by sun-light: the ice blink in the horizon indicates the presence of ice leagues in extent: a seal, killed this day on a piece of ice, was there flayed by the sailors, body left behind: larus eburneus in numbers, and a few of procellaria gulosa.

April 22: ther. 16°, 21°, 20°: wind variable from N.: overcast with cirrostratus: sea level as a lake: ice blink: temperature of air much increased: mild, with cirrostratus variously illuminated, having a rich yellow lustre where it meets the reflected light from the ice: vast numbers of larus eburneus, and P. glacialis following the ship: a pair of the phoca Grœnlandica killed: moon for the first time seen since the change, and surrounded by a broad, somewhat ovate corona.

April 23: ther. 21°, 26°, 29°: wind N. E., fresh breeze: cumulus in long train, with bases pointing southward: cirrostratus in distance accumulated to the sight as if cumulostratus, but is not such: in the course of the forenoon sailed amongst several streams of ice; this sea is called by the whalers "the South West Country:" phoca vitulina, one; P. hispida, two; and P. maculata, one, killed on the ice: in afternoon, some slight nimbus having formed, some snow fell: wind in E. by S. increased to a gale in the night, and after midnight fell to a calm.

April 24: ther. 34°, 42°, 33°: wind S., strong breeze: atmosphere filled with light milky haze; patches of brown cirrostratus; this sea lies east of the entrance to Hudson's Bay: a heavy swell from the S. E.

April 25: ther. 33°, descending to 19½°: wind N. N. E., strong

with which those rocks seemed to be covered, the late winter must have been very severe. Queen Anne's Cape is an island advancing very forward, and forms a common wing to two fine adjacent bays. The land northward of this Cape is not nearly so elevated as that above mentioned.

gale: snow falling thick, light and soft: fucus palmatus drifted past: many birds around: three small islands seen, and rocks over which the sea broke with fury: the fucus warned the people of this danger: the atmosphere so dense with cloud as to prevent a view of land: at noon an observation being taken lat. 64° 24′ N. proved the islands seen to be to the northward of Baal's River mouth, a most dangerous coast, as a great indraught is known about the entrance to that river, and against which mariners are constantly cautioned:* the islands seen lay N. E. of the sunken rock: the snow fell in increased quantity, and of singular shape, thin, pellucid, icy; generally from a centre, six radii extend themselves; the adjoined is an accurate sketch.

April 26: ther. 18°, 20°, 23°: wind N. N. E., light breeze: cirrostratus in loose masses: many species of larus: a shoal of balœna physalus passed in view; some of very great length: afternoon remarkably fine: land at Baal's River seen: very lofty peaked summits covered with snow: lat. by observation 64° 14′ N.

April 27: ther. 23°, 30°, 28°: wind N. E., fresh breeze: the wind unfavourable for a passage: the high snowy peaks of Greenland in view about forty miles distant: beautiful undulate and comoid cirrus in the zenith: cirrostratus lower, and cumulus in the horizon scattered amongst a milky stratus: cumulostratus in N. W. indicates wind: cirrostratus lying far below the lofty summits of the mountains: water lying on the ship's deck

* It is thought the "London," a whale ship, was lost somewhere about this dreadful coast.

On the 6th of May we passed Reef Koll at one p. m. The latitude of this island seems not to be accurately laid down upon the chart, which is serious, as it is the great beacon for the whale ships going to the northward. The upper strata of the rock of Reef Koll bear the appearance of basalt deep-

and no appearance of freezing: colymbus troile seen: lat. ob. 64° 23′ N.

April 28: ther. 27°, 30°, 27°, wind N. by W., light breeze: various modifications of cirrostratus, heavy, still, and dark: land distant ten leagues, and some islands with low conic tops. The setting sun flung his radii from an abrupt collection of cirrostratus, the field being richest yellow: cumulus inclining the summit to N. E.: moon surrounded with halo: some portions of iridescence visible: trichecus rosmarus seen: lat. 64° 41′.

April 29: ther. 27° throughout: wind N. E., strong breeze: cirrostratus overcast, discharging small soft snow: colymbus troile and anas mollissima numerous.

April 30: ther. 19°, 22°, 19°: wind variable about N.: strong tide stream: loose ice much worn: cirrostratus: lat. observed 64° 44′ N.

May 1: ther. 26°, 28°, 26°: wind S. E., light breeze: diffuse cirrostratus covers the welkin: ice blink is observable towards N. W.: air temperate and pleasant: numerous trains of colymbus troile: some snow: the atmosphere having cleared, the land to the southward of Cape Monkchese came in view: there was a constant view of the land all this day: at 8 p. m. passed Queen Anne's Cape: meridian observation gave lat. 65° 56′ N. Sheets of ice, of recent congelation, lay around the ship in her course during this afternoon, composed of pieces six or eight inches over, nearly circular, the interstices being filled up with similar small ones: the wind always fell as the ship came up with those sheets.

May 2: ther. 19°, 22°, 18°: wind N. E., strong breeze: this wind being contrary, the ship continued tacking off and on be-

ly tinged with iron: lower down it deepens to greenish blue, with an irregularity, but sharpness of fracture, like that of the rock, clink basalt, on which stands the castle of Edinburgh.

The island of Disko, called by the natives Duskee, is visible from Reef Koll. At a distance of twenty miles it seemed not far remote. It is table land, the

fore the land just N. of Queen Anne's Cape: the cold intense: vast streams of ice sometimes in sight: since noon the weather became excessively cloudy: sea, rudely high, covered the deck with foam, which immediately became ice, to the great annoyance of the sailors: wind at times violent: masses of ice covering the sea: the pieces of young ice much more minute than those observed the preceding day: a few of P. glacialis seen.

May 3: ther. 15°, 18°, 16°: wind N. E., fresh breeze increasing: ship standing off and on by land: the dip of the rock hereabouts seems to be about an angle of 60° N. and S.: no birds seen: in the latter part, continual snow shower, with sharpest cold: the wind continued in the same point a strong gale all the day: lat. obs. 66° 38′ North.

May 4: ther. 10°, 12°, 13°: wind N. E., strong breeze: the cold increased this day to a distressing degree. The Wild Islands, with numerous rocks near them, both not far distant from the coast, came into view: the fracture of the rock appeared very sharp: the colour and smoothness near the water gave it a resemblance to greenstone: numerous flocks of the anas mollissima, colymbus troile, and of the genus larus around in every direction: much scattered ice: the atmosphere generally very clear.

May 5: ther. 10°, 22°, 18°: wind S. E., fresh breeze: ship standing in close with the land, which no longer presented the angular prominences of the lands more to the southward: this lies low with rounded summits, but no appearance of plain: after passing through streams of ice, and by bergs of the most fantastic forms, the ship was made fast to a berg, at a short distance from the shore, in about ten fathoms water: saw this day a solitary ra-

interior parts more elevated than the southern side, and scarcely swells above a plane. On the 7th of May, every part, but the steep faces of the rock, was covered with snow, which also lay upon the debris of the mountain: the parts however next the water were bare of snow. From the great distance at which it first becomes visible above the horizon, this island must be more than a mile in perpendicular height. The face of the rock is torn in channels for the discharge of the dissolved snow, which, as they grow narrower in their descent, give the spaces between the appearance of stupendous pyramids, a resemblance which is much heightened by the stratification exhibiting horizontal and parallel fissure, similar to regular building. The rock is basaltic, but not of that regular form which occurs in the Giants' Cause-

ven, great numbers of Eider ducks, and some seals; the latter being remarkably cautious of observation: the state of cloud was uniformly haze: the tide here is amazingly rapid: islands around; these are the Wild Islands.

May 6: ther. 17°, 36°, 21°: wind S., fresh breeze: ship cast off from the berg, and proceeding to the northward: sounding near the land ten fathoms: twenty-one ships in sight: this day heard of the melancholy loss of the London with all her crew: a light stratus is the only cloud in view: atmosphere agreeably mild: immense flocks of ducks on wing; hereabouts is their favourite haunt for rearing their young. About 8 p. m. passed the western islands, which lie low and very flat, much inhabited by the natives: Disko in sight, appearing high above the horizon: saw flocks of colymbus grylle, also a raven: immense numbers of procellaria glacialis making rapid flight to the north-westward.

May 7: ther. 25°, 30°, 25°: wind S. E., strong breeze.

way. Its height is sixty feet. There are parts however where the stratification is much more regular.

These remarks chiefly regard the south side about Fortune Bay, which seems to be that part of this island which has been least affected by that awful convulsion which at some remote period denudated and destroyed this portion of the globe. Probably the ruin that came upon these countries moved, in its terrible progress, from the north-westward; and, having forced a passage through the Waygat Strait, swept round through the southeast bay, and so spared Disko. In support of such conjecture, it may be advanced, that Hare Island, lying nearly north of Disko, at the entrance to Waygat Sound, is low and flat, as it were the base of a mountain whose summit had been torn away. The contiguous point of Disko shelves into the sea, as if having suffered from the same cause: whilst that side of Disko that overlooks the Waygat consists of lofty peaks, behind which there lie deep valleys, where the torrent rioted, having failed to carry away the more elevated parts. Moreover, that part of Disko called Flat Foot Shore, which lies over against Makkely Onit, has evidently suffered during the same devastation. Neither would that portion of the island called New and Old Lievely have survived the wreck, were it not for the strong resistance made by that part which is known by the name of the Black Land. The rock of Lievely, now so dangerous to navigators, which is bare at low water spring tides, and which is nothing but the remains of some part of the mountain, is a further proof of the justice of the above assertion. The existence of Disko Bay, Fortune Bay, Love Bay, and the other recesses in the bosom of this remarkable rock, owe their existence to the violence of the flood which, boiling at the resistance opposed to it on the north side, rushed over the higher lands to the southward, and there pouring onward, in its rage hollowed out those several bays, and meeting with the other contending currents coming through the Waygat, and down the Straits, completed the work of destruction, and effected the formation of South East Bay.

CHAPTER II.

OF THE STATE OF GREENLAND, AS INSULAR, OR CONTINENTAL.

Having conducted the reader thus far along this dreary coast, and this part of the subject being appropriate to our purpose, I shall here beg leave to take into consideration the actual state of the countries called Greenland; chiefly with a view to inquire whether that state be insular or continental.

Spitzbergen, or New or East Greenland, has been already determined by Lord Mulgrave to be an island. So far the necessity is removed of alluding further to that portion of these lands. The whale fisheries, as they are called, when spoken of as the Greenland fisheries, are always carried on to the westward of Spitzbergen, and usually so that the vessels in that trade often have a view of some part of that island in the course of the season. Westward of the fishing ground, the perpetual ice presents an insurmountable barrier to any attempt to explore the eastern coast of West or Old Greenland above a certain degree, where Herjolf's Ness, in the sixty-third degree, forms a bold round promontory. It is not recorded that any navigator has penetrated further north than this point on the eastern side, though some charts exhibit inlets bearing Dutch or Danish names somewhat higher up. We may, therefore, fairly assume it as a fact, that

Greenland on the eastern side from Herjolf's Ness to the pole is decidedly unexplored, and the reports of experienced seamen are positive in expressing the impossibility of coming within many degrees of the supposed line of coast from the continual presence of ice; and that the ice which is carried to the southward from the Greenland fishing grounds is always limited to a certain meridian, westward of which it has been never known to break up. Eastward of this parallel they have at times penetrated beyond the eighty-fourth degree.

South and westward of Herjolf's Ness is Skagafiord, a sound, the termination of which was never ascertained; but from its apparent direction, it is thought to have a communication with Makkely Onit in South-East Bay, at Disko.

Between Herjolf's Ness and Staten Hook there were many more inlets inhabited in former times. Whether these inlets may not have a leading into the preceding communication, must not be looked upon as at variance with probability.

No one now will doubt that Frobisher's Straits penetrate the whole of southern Greenland, or rather open into some vast internal sea, whence the ice is annually carried westward, so as to obstruct the entrance to those parts from the side of Hudson's Bay.

Staten Hook, also the most southern extremity of Greenland, and Cape Farewell, the south-western extremity, have been both determined to be islands, between which there lies an immense bay, crowded with islands. The bottom of this, never having been yet explored, may be supposed to have many inlets branching into Frobisher's Straits.

Let us turn our attention to Baal's River, which is rather a gulf penetrating Greenland to the N. E. The extremity of this water has not been as yet laid down. It is supposed to extend to Disko by some inlet leading into South-East Bay. In its length it is impossible to deny but it may have communication with Skagafiord, and the inland waters in Frobisher's Straits.

Whether South Bay is connected with Baal's River is not easy to assert, as there is no datum for such an assertion.

Makkely Onit in South-East Bay has been always allowed as running into a water, which, if free from ice, would permit a passage into the northern Atlantic.

North of Makkely Onit are numerous passages opening into internal seas in the northern parts of Greenland, some of which have been penetrated by the boats of the whale hunters, the men of which, on their return, invariably reported that they had observed fair, open seas before them after they had gone a very little way.

In Jacob's Bay there is one very remarkable passage of similar description; so also one, if not more, in North-East Bay; and proceeding further north, the numerous sounds up to the Women's Islands and forward to the Devil's Thumb, an isolated natural column, in 74° 53′ north latitude, various openings present themselves, which, no doubt, lead to so many ways of traversing this Arctic Archipelago.

A few circumstances more will materially assist in this inquiry. The whale hunters are unanimously of opinion that Greenland consists entirely of islands; "for," say they, "wherever chance or inclination led us, on almost any part of the coast, we saw nothing to prevent us from sailing as far inwards as we liked." The habits of the whale, who is observed always running for some one or other of those passages, and some, when stricken, dragging the boats so far that the people witnessed open clear water to a boundless extent, are in a great degree confirmatory evidence of the fact. But one circumstance, not the least curious in natural history, is, that a whale, struck by a man at Greenland, i. e. at Spitzbergen, escaped, and was in a short time after killed, and taken by a relative of the same man, who was then at Davis's Straits. This curious fact was determined by the harpoon, bearing the mark of the former, being found in the body of the animal when taken.

The north-east coast of Greenland, therefore, being unexplored, and the probable intersection of its south-eastern, southern, western, and north-western parts, by navigable waters being adduced, besides the other circumstances, in aid, it may, I presume, be inferred, that the state of Greenland is not continental but insular. But whether the research will be ever established by future proofs of more decisive character, or whether any circumstances will warrant the hazard, must be left for time to determine.

CHAPTER III.

OF THE NATIVES OF GREENLAND.

The description of savage life is nearly alike applicable to almost every portion of mankind placed below a certain degree of refinement. The necessary means to prolong life are so varied by chance, convenience, or choice, in different nations, that what is familiarly called comfort becomes invested with a thousand meanings when used as descriptive of comparative happiness. The poor Greenlander, feasting on his raw food, is as truly happy in such luxury as the citizen of a more indulgent climate who is uneasy in his armed chair until he has the delight of gloting over his pudding, a seventh dish at his usual dinner. In the humble, yet happy, people that are found in the high northern latitudes, and are generally known by the name of the Esquimeaux, more of that spirit of contentment, which is the genuine offspring of necessity, is discernible than probably in any other class of mankind whatsoever.

It is not the material of satiety that constitutes what is generally estimated as domestic comfort. So far as the mere necessaries of life are considered in relation to this, the Palais Royal is perhaps as scanty as the hut of the Esquimeaux. The Tartar who bestrides his dinner, which, to save time and cookery, is placed within his saddle skirts, looks to an enjoyment of relish equally fine to his taste as the double repast of turtle is to the Liverpool merchant. Embrowned in his dreary retreat, the Greenlander feels no inconvenience, unless the accidental severity of the weather forbid his accustomed seal-hunting; and should this blessing, with the other casualties of his better fortune, come opportunely and in plenty, it may be very truly asserted, that he envies not the lot of any fellow mortal.

The influence of climate has been frequently referred to as a source of those distinctions that mark the various tribes of mankind. No person in the present period will venture, one would suppose, to produce another Adam as the progenitor from whom the coppery savage of America would claim a distinct descent, rather than attribute his singular complexion and warlike character to the influence of local circumstances. The wants and hardships which his forefathers have known, and the severe but necessary exertions to overcome those difficulties, must have produced strong and permanent constitutional effects, growing more into character by succeeding years, and on its transmission to posterity always increased. As an exposition of this principle, the difference of manners already between the United States' American and his British predecessors, has become very strongly marked; and little doubt can be entertained but that in the progress of several centuries the North American colonist will be as remote in habits and general character from the European as both at present stand in geographical situation.

The vast population of the northern regions of the earth, has been long a matter of surprise. The destruction of the eastern empires, China, for instance, and that of India, from the irruption of the Tartar hordes, are memorable proofs of the population of the North having been in early times amazingly great. The ruin of the Roman empire followed from the same cause; and, in a later period, the world has witnessed the annihilation of one of the most warlike armies that ever was known, by the descendants of those very Tartars.

There may be assumed a line embracing the globe to be considered as an equator of civilization, towards which, as man approximates, his faculties are observed to be more perfectly developed; whilst on the other hand, receding from this equator, some of the higher and more beautiful portions of human character die away. Ancient Greece would appear to be traversed by this line. Here the finest specimens of man in full possession of his faculties, in refinement of manners, language, and the arts, have existed; and if the moderns have surpassed the inhabitants of ancient Greece in aught, they have had the lights of the ancients to direct them. The Divine wisdom displayed in the New Testament is another splendid proof of the truth of the position above assumed. It appeared among mankind diffusing benevolence and peace to all the nations of the earth from a spot within the limits laid down.

This line, however, is not always unbroken, but is subject to variations arising from localities, which must ever exercise a predominant influence over mankind. We may also notice that it is not at variance with the general laws of nature that differences may arise subject to such influence. The line by which the mariner's needle is directed to the north is not always steadily noted by the magnet. The variation of the compass, the irregular motions of the needle, sometimes in the vicinity of mountains, and often where the land is very little elevated, are evidence that circumstances will cause a deviation from a universally established rule. Perhaps it is to some unseen cause that the great diversity of human character is to be attributed; and some persons will insist that half the happiness of life depends upon that very diversity.

Situation has a surprising effect also on the human constitution and character. The inhabitant of the mountain differs essentially from the inhabitant of the plain; their pursuits and passions are widely different. The one is all energy, activity, and simplicity; the other comparatively gross, plodding, and inactive. The mountaineer, striding over his hills, is roused to action by the gust that shakes the oak above his slumber; a light meal fits him for the toils of hardy life; and in the quick ardent glance, and sinewy step, are evolved those energies derived to him from his situation, and which he fancies have descended to him from his sire. Rarely, however, is such a situation the nursery of science. It is in the champaign country that the historian will find the origin of all those arts by which modern society is now so much improved.

The early dispersion of mankind could not have

been attended with those remarkable effects all at once. Centuries must have passed before the various ramifications could drop into separate nations; and climate, situation, and habits must have exercised their powers long before national distinctions could be recognised. The tide of population descending into the more temperate regions, spread over the limits of Europe, and filled it with a race of men who were equally removed from the enervating softness of Asiatic climate, and the more severe and chilling influence of frost. On this point rests the main distinction.

Heat, as has been before observed, when in excess, produces effects similar to those of excessive cold. Hence, as population is traced north or south from a certain assumed line, the high, august forehead, the erect figure, and calm majestic deportment, recede and dwindle. The African exhibits the organs of sense largely developed—patulous nostrils, large lips and mouth, prominent eyes—all proportionally increased; whilst, in the same degree, the internal organs of the mind become diminished, until the character is scarcely above that of idiocy. The social affections are, under such circumstances, extremely weak, and consequently the progress of civilization is visibly embarrassed. But as the cold of northern regions can be mitigated by artificial means, the situation of the Laplander or Samoëide is consequently less in extreme than that of the inhabitant of the torrid zone, who is perpetually exposed to a burning sun. In the manners and tempers of both there is a manifest distinction. Ferocious, vengeful, and rapacious, the African will allow nothing to thwart his resistless passion; whilst on the contrary the Arctic Tartar, humble and simple, is content with his dreary wastes and precarious subsistence, seldom raising his mind to the attractions of revolution.

The early discoverers of Greenland were surprised to meet with a people already in possession of those countries. They described them as diminutive in person, dressed in skins, and moving about in little boats covered also with skins. They are represented as not having ships; and yet subsequent adventurers from Europe met tribes of this same people both in Newfoundland and the waters north of that place, and also in Greenland.

That this description exactly suits the natives of Greenland at the present day will not be disputed; but it must appear singular, that a people confessedly aboriginal in those inhospitable regions, should, after a lapse of nearly two thousand years, be found the same in every respect at the present day, as they appeared to the first European voyagers.

Charlevoix, a French historian of much accuracy, states their national appellation to be Esquimeaux, which is a word of their own language having a French termination. This writer explains the term as meaning "eaters of raw flesh;" but to this interpretation some objections may be reasonably made. For instance, would any people be found desirous to stigmatize themselves with a nickname? One only reply to this can appear satisfactory, which is, that they might give themselves such a name to mark the superiority, as they may conceive, of their own nation above every other, in their being able to partake of the fruits of their hunting on the spot, whilst the other must perish unless he have the unnecessary luxury of cooking. The value of this observation, however, is much diminished, when it is known that the Greenlander, though he can eat his food undressed, and generally does so, by no means would prefer that mode to the greater comfort of having his dinner in the European manner; but he is, in a great degree, compelled to adopt the former custom of necessity; and the effects arising from custom are well known to infuse themselves into the constitution, and produce what is generally denominated habit. Ellis relates a story of a youth who had been carried away from his native country, and, on his return, the sailors having killed a seal, he eagerly seized a portion of the raw flesh and ate it, expressing his delight at finding a circumstance which so strongly brought to mind his dear native country.

The fact, however, is, that the national appellation by which these people distinguish themselves from others is not Esquimeaux, as has been so long received, but is by themselves pronounced in quite a different manner. Were I to write it, as I observed it spoken by them, it should be Uskeemè; (pronounced according to our sounds oos-kè-mà;) and of this appellation they are as proud as a native of this country is of the name of Briton. Any person desirous of obtaining their immediate attention and civility, should address them with the term Uskee, which never fails to ensure that respectful regard which is shown by conciliated minds. The English sailors indulge in their usual humour of abbreviating names, and have not refrained from exercising their ingenuity in reducing Uskee into Yak, which ingenuity, however, has not afforded much satisfaction to the natives. Probably by similar means the North American Yankee has been invented.

From these remarks it must be apparent that there is not much dependence to be put on the explanation given by Charlevoix as to their national name. He says, that Abenaqui Esquimantsic signifies eater of raw flesh, and that they are the only nation in the world that eats raw flesh; but the accounts of many Tartar tribes are positive in asserting, that the eating of raw flesh is known and practised in many parts of northern Tartary, and that the Tartar horseman usually has no other mode of preparing his repast than by placing it on his horse's back beneath the saddle, which practice cannot be looked upon as a refinement in cookery. Hence it is evident that the Greenlanders, or Uskee-mè tribes, must have received their national name from some other cause.

In all the revolutions that language has undergone, the pronoun seems to have maintained a sort of inviolability throughout all nations. This is very remarkable in the present case, in which the personal pronoun, belonging to the speaker, is obviously the same as in other languages. Thus, when an Uskee wishes to express absolute refusal, he says, na-me, i.e. not for me. Requesting the reader to bear this in mind, I shall next mention that the old Roman term for water is written asqua; and, as it is evidently a remnant of an original language carried from the East in the course of colonization, it will not be overstrained to find its use adopted by other people very far remote from the theatre of the Latin tongue. Another term in the language just mentioned is the word cunnus, signifying woman, the "belli teterrima causa" of the satirist. The reader will probably be somewhat surprised to find a similar term in use among the Greenlanders. The Uskee tells you that the name of his wife is cunà. Besides, the old Latin word cunabula, cradle, has a relative term in the language of the Uskee-mè, cuna-bla-bush, coitus.

Taking notice, therefore of the word asqua, water, and applying it to the term Uskee, it requires very little aid of the imagination to find a close analogy. This analogy is supported by the fact, that these people are nowhere found but in the vicinity of water. From it they draw subsistence; and its presence must be ever foremost in their thoughts, and naturally lead them to designate their nation peculiarly by some term, in which water must bear a prominent share. The adjunct of mè gives additional force to this observation, as the moment an Uskee-mè makes his appearance amongst them, though previously an entire stranger, he is hailed with joy by this name, and is therefore entitled to all the rights of hospitality.

Before we come to speak of their manners and customs, it may not be amiss to attempt an inquiry as to their original residence. In this respect, it is best to consider them exclusively as fishermen, as they are seldom known to stray a day's journey from the shore inland. It is true, indeed, they sometimes go in pursuit of deer; but as on the American side such pursuit would lead them into the neighbourhood of nations hostile to them, and consequently produce less or more the reduction of their numbers, which they are most careful to avoid, they are very unwilling to expose themselves to such hazard, and content themselves with what they can procure from the sea. In Greenland, however, there must be deer, more particularly towards the south. It is rare in those islands to see any animal of that description, and deer-skin is seldom seen to form a part of their dress. The Danes, indeed, may deprive them of such skins, by inducing the poor creatures to barter with their masters; and hence the rare occurrence of seeing an Uskee furnished with any portion of deer-skin. In Hudson's Bay, the name for a deer is, according to writers who have given accounts of that country, tuk-toa; and in Greenland the same is pronounced more softly, and may be written tu-tu (too too.) The trifling difference of sound in this instance is nothing: and it is mentioned as tending to identify the people who inhabit Greenland and Hudson's Bay. There can be no doubt of their having a common origin, being in size, customs and pursuits, precisely on the same scale.

In person they are diminutive, but stoutly made. They seldom stand above four feet four inches, except in Greenland, where the national figure is changed by intermarriage with the Danes. The native Uskees do not cordially associate with this mixed race, which they consider as degenerate. In complexion, they are generally of an olive-brown. Their forehead and the sides of the head, above the temples, are greatly depressed; the crown is elevated considerably; and the back of the head is depressed, as the forehead. The smaller end of a hen's egg presents a familiar resemblance to their cranium. Their eyes are usually small, but piercing, not brilliant; and the calm mild manner with which they contemplate a stranger gives a good idea of the power of their eye. Their vision is astonishingly strong, by means of which they can distinguish objects at an incredible distance. The snow glare affects their eyes very much, which are often observed to be inflamed.—Against this inconvenience, they have many ingenious contrivances, in the manner of eye-shades, which are usually a piece of wood made to fit across the eyes, having two fine slits, and a pinhole in the centre of each to correspond to the centre of vision. Their cheek bones are high, which, with their rounded flabby cheeks, renders the nose by no means a prominent feature. Their lips and mouth are generally large; the former very much protruded. The lower part of their face altogether forms a striking contrast to their narrow forehead, and is a chief distinguishing feature of this people. The women differ little from the men, except that they are not so tall. Their hands are remarkably fine, small, and neat. The same remark applies with regard to their feet.

The dress of both sexes is nearly alike, the women being distinguished only by their jacket terminating in a triangular piece, before and behind, reaching nearly to the knees. Nothing about the persons of the Uskee-mès is more remarkable than their hair.

It hangs from their poll, long, black, coarse and lank, exactly like the hairy parts of the whalebone. The women tie it in a bunch upon the top of the head, which takes away much of the unsightliness of such an object.

Having stated so much regarding the person of the Greenlander, we shall proceed to trace him in his emigration.

That they are of Tartar origin, may be very fairly assumed. Their general cast of feature, their retired and cautious habits, and above all their unconquerable disposition to change their place of abode, are evident proofs of this assumption being correct. In this view, then, some of them may be considered as having moved westward, and colonized Lapland, where they are found in boats of the same construction as those of the Greenlander and Hudson's Bay Esquimeaux, and devoted to the very same pursuits. Others proceeding northward and eastward, peopled the Samoëid country, and whether by accident or design, ventured across Behring's Straits,* which, considering their surprising dexterity in the management of their little boats, was not at all difficult to effect. Besides, on an expedition of this nature they are never unemployed. The ice, which covers that Strait at certain times, serves as a place of repose to the seals, which may be truly termed the live stock of the Greenlander. These animals, therefore, in the course

* Behring, in his voyage, found the small islands lying across the Straits peopled by Esquimeaux, for such they appeared by their dress and manners.

of the expedition, become a certain resource against famine; as every part of the seal is turned to account—the very intestines being usefully employed by way of floats attached to the darts. The women, too, who are never left behind when a removal is carried on, will, during such a voyage, convert the seal or bird skins into convenient dresses, so that this little roving tribe are seldom at a loss, the sea supplying all their wants. Should an extensive field of ice present itself, they at once get out of their boats, each man takes his kajak on his head; the women must look after their umiak; (the names of the fishing and family boats;) and, in this manner they traverse immense fields of ice, which saves the labour of paddling round them, and, of course, shortens their journey very considerably. Such is their patience under toil, when seated in their boats upon their favourite element, that they usually perform the distance of twenty leagues a day. That is the way in which they describe a day's rowing in a kaiak. In this manner it is very plain that they might have passed along the arctic shores of North America; and if the conjecture be plausible, they might, year after year, have extended themselves through the numerous waters that are sprinkled over that unexplored region, exulting in the solitudes they met with, and which to them were secure blessings.

Thus have they, in the course of their emigration, passed from Siberia into America, and spread themselves over all the shores of North America to the eastward, always settling upon low islands, contiguous to the best waters for killing seals and wild fowl, &c.: a people so accustomed to hardy fare could not be much at a loss to find a residence on such a coast, whence the passage to Greenland was not difficult. The latter, however, must have been attended with much difficulty and danger. But that it has been effected is undoubtedly true, as the first European adventurers found them in possession of that country in the tenth century. So also about that period they were found as far south as Newfoundland. There must consequently have elapsed a great number of years before they could have advanced so far southward; and, of course, their emigration must have commenced at a period previous to the Christian era.

In the course of their wanderings, coming in contact with other tribes, who from causes, not necessary to form a part of this inquiry, had already spread over other parts of the American continent, and being of peaceful and very unwarlike habits, they were unfit to associate with their new neighbours. The consequence was, that the red Indians, as they are termed, who lived entirely by the chase, usually attributed to their timid neighbours every unfavourable change of weather that interfered with their hunting. Hence arose wars, which to the present day are continued with undiminished asperity. The appearance too of the Uskee, clad in his skins, his head wrapped in a hood, and his whole figure lowly, and little expressive of warlike character, was remarkably contrasted with the tall, graceful figure of the red man, accustomed to warfare, and impatient of intrusion.

The Uskees, in self-defence, must have learned also how to fight, and doubtless retaliated with devastating effect, having always a sure retreat in their boats.

This disposition the early settlers from Norway found to their cost, when they provoked them to vengeance in Greenland, and were in consequence extirpated. Neither did a subsequent visit from the Europeans tend to diminish the rancour arising from unprovoked injury. For, in the year 1605, Christian IV. of Denmark having sent out Admiral Lindenow with a small fleet, under the guidance of John Knight, an English mariner, in search of Old Greenland, "they seized four wild men, and were obliged to kill one of them to render the others tractable;" a most extraordinary specimen truly of European refinement.

In the settlement of Newfoundland and Canada by the English and French, those Uskees who had ventured so far south, and had been there established for centuries, finding the strangers determined on retaining possession of the country, unanimously resolved to abandon those shores, which they accordingly did; and have since fixed their abode in the northern parts of Hudson's Bay, and among the lakes and seas in the northern parts of North America, where they now remain unmolested, except by some of their warlike neighbours from the southward and westward.

Mr. Ellis states that the severity of the cold beyond the sixty-first degree causes the trees to dwindle into brushwood, and that none of the human species appeared beyond the sixty-seventh degree, inferring that human life could not sustain the cold beyond that degree. This applies, in Mr. Ellis's account, to the natives around the bottom of Hudson's Bay; but the shores northward and north-westward of that degree remain to be satisfactorily explored; in which event it will certainly be found that Uskees inhabit countries of much higher latitudes than the sixty-seventh. On the Greenland side of Davis's Straits it was supposed that no natives existed beyond the sixty-fourth degree; but subsequent research found them numerous along the coast as far as Disko. Here discovery seemed to terminate; but not long after, other navigators met with a population sprinkled over the low islands up to the seventy-third degree, where the voyagers saw many women in boats, and traded with them for seal skins, and unicorns' horns. It is a positive fact, moreover, that they have been met with at the Devil's Thumb, in the seventy-fifth degree nearly, provided with muskets. How much further north they can be traced is doubtful; but that they can exist beyond the degree stated by Mr. Ellis is without question. Hence also arises a presumption that the cold in those high latitudes is not of such severity as to forbid living there through the winter, particularly if due precaution be observed.

At Disko, or rather at Lievely, there is a Danish settlement, where a factor constantly resides, and lives very comfortably. The Danish government maintains a governor for the superintendence and management of their concerns in that quarter, who constantly resides there. Buffon hazarded an opinion that there was no ice at the pole, grounding his conjecture on the supposed warmth of the atmosphere in that place; but this part of the subject shall be taken into consideration more fully, when we come to discuss the question of a north-west passage.

The Danes, in re-establishing their claims to the

possession of Greenland, have done very little towards ameliorating the condition of the natives. The natural disposition however of the Uskees, Gipsey-like, makes them appear to conform to the manners and religion of their masters; yet little doubt of their insincerity exists. It must be acknowledged that the conduct of many of the Danes sent thither, as it is said, for their crimes, is not well calculated to reconcile them to European sentiments. They are, if spoiled by such corrupt example, looked upon as untractable; and a sensible writer, descanting on their unwillingness to become converted, represents them as listening very attentively to Christian exhortation, and when asked if they understood all that had been said to them, their answer was childishly affirmative, when it was evident they did not comprehend or retain a tittle of the subject. "They are such adepts in disguising or suppressing their passions, that one might take them for stoics in appearance." This short sentence shows very fully their calm and peaceful temper. They never interrupt any person when speaking; and their reply is sensible and brief, and marked with the most respectful deference to the person they address, provided he commands their good opinion. It is when they do not esteem the man, that they are liable to the name of stoics in appearance.

The Danish convicts and settlers have intermarried with the Uskee women, and a mixed generation is now remarkably predominant where the government has been fixed. Some of the children of the Europeans by the Uskee women are quite fair, but all have that remarkable attachment to their country which the genuine natives evince. The young man who amused the people at Hull, Leith, and in the Thames, with the exercise of his kaiak was the son of a Dane, but his mother was a native of Greenland. It is said that the sister of that young man was so much grieved at the thoughts of his going from his dear home that she pined away and died of grief. Such is their excessive attachment to their country.

In their intercourse with strangers, they are at first shy and cautious, but firm in their manners. That reserve soon disappears when they are kindly treated, and they freely communicate their knowledge of any thing asked them. Their experience extending but little beyond the arts befitting the necessary occupations of their own peculiar mode of life, makes their information of inconsiderable value when applied to the greater concerns of European commerce. They appear sensible of their deficiency in this respect; and when they give reply to the inquiries of the whale hunters, it is always frank but diffident. Any effort to extend their experience beyond the contracted circle of their wants, is attended with such a train of imaginary difficulty, that few, if any of them have ever ventured out of the footsteps of their forefathers. The Uskee-mè jacket, trowsers, boots, darts and canoe (for they use this name for a boat indiscriminately with kaiak) are identically the same as they have been observed more than 800 years ago.

The great difficulty of obtaining from these people accurate information respecting the northern countries, is a source of perpetual error and perplexity.

Looking with a jealous eye on all strangers, and tempted by the richness of some paltry present, but which appears in their eyes of much value, they have frequently shown a desire to communicate accounts of their country and its resources, greatly exaggerated, in order to make their information on such subjects appear of the utmost importance to the people from whom such communications were known to bring superior advantages to them. It is a prevailing trait in uncivilized life, to desire strongly such things as come within the direct apprehension of particular wants. This is signally exemplified in the African, who, dead to the calls of consanguinity, is anxious to decorate his graceful neck with a string of Staffordshire ware at the expense of a child; and the wife of his bosom must often be a bit of barter, in order that the human beast may contemplate his perfections in a mirror, in her stead. The same propensity exists in the humble Esquimeaux as in the African; but the desires of the former are finely chastened by a reserve that seems almost peculiar to this people. The tie of consanguinity binds the arctic inhabitant too closely to be unfastened: it is a gordian knot of a texture too refined and complicated to be undone: it is genuine, unsophisticated nature, nursed in the continual presence of all that is dear to existence, and which no temptation can destroy.

There is not probably a nation on the earth more signalized for urbanity than are the inhabitants of Greenland. To witness the splendour of a London assembly, its luxuries, elegance and grandeur, and (were it possible) to turn the eye the next instant on the little patriarchal circle in an Uskee hut, few common minds would relish the comparison; yet to any one accustomed to reflect, and to appreciate the happiness of mankind comparatively, on the scale of necessary wants and wishes, the lot of the apparently wretched Greenlander is far from being miserable. In truth, had European luxury and its allurements been withheld, his state would have still remained in aboriginal simplicity and happiness; and, if any thought arise to disturb his constitutional tranquillity of mind, it proceeds from a reflection that he wants something from the great wak; (it is by this term the Uskee expresses a ship;) and he will readily barter the last article of dress, necessary to the comfort of his person, in order to obtain a bit of lead, or some powder for his gun, or a rag of handkerchief for his cunà.

The commodities generally trafficked with them are such as the sailors find no longer useful to their own accommodation, or some vile coarse articles of dress, of no value when compared with what they get in exchange. In later years, the arts of the European have taught them a little more cunning; and some now are as expert at making a bargain as any of their visiters. In this respect, they compliment the honour of the English very pointedly in contrast with the conduct of the Danes. They frequently say, "Englishman good, Uskee good, Danskee no good," thereby leaving an inference that they are by no means, even yet, satisfied with the presence of strangers, and consider the blessings which their master would communicate, greatly under the value of their natural inheritance. Strictly honest in all their dealings, they are also exceedingly watchful that they be not cheated; and he must indeed be worse than savage who would wrong people of such direct integrity as they are remarkable for. The hardships and perils through which they must toil in order to procure material articles for barter, should also form a humane consideration of their condition, and protect them from injustice. Some serious grounds, therefore, of dislike towards the Danish dominancy, must exist, before these people, strongly guided by a sense of right and wrong, could be brought to express an abhorrence of their master's principles; and this must be either by the Danes exacting from their industry a demand in the shape of tax for the protection afforded them, or for the support of the missionaries, or else by trucking with them on terms obviously disadvantageous to the natives. On either point, the Uskee feels his superiority in principle over his master, and is not to be reconciled to his views.

The original form of society still exists amongst the Uskee-mès in all its simplicity. Though a nation as distinctly defined as any other in the world, yet they are such only in identity of character. Their institutions are truly patriarchal without the danger of dissolution from the extravagant acquisition of property. Whilst in the early government of patriarchal form, the gradual accession of landed property and flocks of cattle and servants led to the despotism of some wealthier lord; and many, sharing such abundance in common, desired a chief who should maintain equal justice, these petty governments became gradually absorbed into larger ones, and empires have been formed, and revolutions given rise to ruinous and wasting wars. During all this, that has formed the basis of ancient and modern history, the simple Uskeemè, content in his kaiak, plies his paddle in unmolested waters, kills his seals and wild birds, or transfixes his nimbler game, and in the bosom of his small rejoicing family enjoys his good fortune, and trains his son to imitate the prowess and skill of his sire. Living in a manner that requires little from the neighbouring soil, he farms not, he tills not, nor concerns himself in the slightest degree about the right of property in the territory in which he resides: he is consequently free of the broils which such species of property is likely to create. Give him his fishing waters, and leave him undisturbed, "he takes no thought for the morrow."

The father of a family is to all intents absolute chief; but still his authority is exercised with the mildest sway. To chide for a fault is considered the severest punishment. Blows are never resorted to. It is considered a savage and barbarous act to strike an Uskee, and is looked on with abhorrence. The women are treated kindly, but are regarded as servants, doing all the labours of the house, excepting such parts as the men think their superior understanding only can be equal to. Domestic harmony is seldom known to be disturbed, unless when in the absence of the men some dowager mother exercises her peevishness upon her daughter-in-law, especially if the latter have not the good fortune to have been the mother of a son; for on the birth of male children they think the existence of the nation rests.

The men are the carpenters; the women the tailors, shoemakers, house-masons, and cooks, the last more particularly, as the men, on returning with game, no sooner are disengaged from their kaiaks than all further concern on their part ceases. This arises very probably from the excessive fatigue to which they have been exposed, rather than to any indifference towards their women. The women's labour then commences. They have to haul the seals ashore, and convey to the tent or hut the different animals taken. Their first concern being to draw a little blood from the seal, (which, after being killed, is stanched for that purpose,) and present it to the men, by way of cordial after their fatigue. Then, having provided the men with dry clothes, they proceed to flay and cut up the spoil. Seal's flesh forms their chief support; and they employ various modes of preserving it for future use. The most common is to cut it into thin slips, and so dry it over a line in the interior of their huts. The blubber is most carefully preserved, as being convertible to almost every domestic comfort, more precious by far to them than wine is to others. Oil is the luxury of their meals, their bread being nothing more than the dried muscular part of the seals or of birds.

Such a representation of life would form little inducement to a European to exchange his comforts in its room. The picture is to such appetites truly disgusting; and the horrible smell of their huts, persons, and almost every article belonging to them, is intolerable to the coarsest feeling. Even the sailor accustomed to the atmosphere of a whale-ship has been frequently known to nauseate the inside of a Greenlander's hut. Those poor creatures smile at such squeamishness, and kindly excuse the want of politeness in the stranger, as he could not possibly know any thing better.

The whale often wounded, and carrying in his huge body the instrument of destruction, very often in his anguish runs himself ashore, or into some creek among the rocks, and there, lingering, dies. Such a chance is an unexpected blessing if discovered; and any person who has ever winded a dead whale must know that an occurrence of that kind is not likely to remain long a secret. Every hut is then emptied to take advantage of the fortunate occasion. If any one is within reach of the good tidings, he is immediately invited, and it is easy to imagine what a scene ensues. Men, women, and children, with every edged instrument at command, are in full employment. But in such eagerness wounds are often inflicted by accident, and such are never resented. The blubber is carefully stored, that it may subside into oil; the muscular parts are removed for future fare, and nothing can be of coarser texture, yet still they relish it, and are thankful for the blessing. The tendons also are carefully preserved, to be appropriated as cordage, thread, lines, and for various other purposes; and in the whalebone they have sufficient for their own private necessities, and for the demands of the Danes.

In winter time they retire further from the sea than they had been in the summer months, and in their huts or winter houses generally spend the interval between the latter end of October and the middle of March in getting up their fishing tackle, whilst the women are busily engaged in repairing the kaiak, or sewing dresses for the men. On such occasions the children have an opportunity of learning the arts peculiar to their sex, and scarcely any other time is given for their education.

As soon as the returning sun announces the approach of summer, all is bustle and activity. The materials for the summer huts are got in readiness, and the whole household, sometimes consisting of five or six families, moves downwards to the fishing place, which is generally a low island with a sloping beach looking towards the south, for the ease and convenience of launching the boats or drawing the seals ashore. They are not confined to any particular spot for the summer: unless abundance of seals be seen, they generally shift to some other station, which in the course of former seasons they have observed as more fit, or as they may have information from others of their countrymen.

The Greenlander is very vain of his accomplishments; and viewing them, as he does, as the perfection of human art, he pities the ignorance of any one who is unable to manage a kaiak, or use the hand-board in discharging the spear or lighter dart. It is dangerous for a European to venture into one of those canoes, as he is almost certain of being instantly upset, in which case the buoyancy of the little bark would certainly keep him immersed, and drown him.

The seal, mischievous in the extreme towards every

creature weaker than himself, entertains a sovereign dread of the Uskee-mè, and flies from every quarter where he discovers a kaiak; but his precaution seldom avails. The instant a seal is seen by a Greenlander, he whispers "pussee" (seal) along the surface of the water to the nearest of his companions, who telegraphs the signal until all the boats are engaged in the chase, and it is seldom possible for their prey to escape. The seal is impetuous in disposition, and, having once observed his pursuers, he dives repeatedly, and in different directions, to confound them; but becomes at length so short-winded by his hurry, that he cannot remain long out of sight; and as the Uskees are around in various points watching the favourable moment, one of them paddles silently in his rear, using the paddle with one hand, whilst with the other he is getting his tackle in order; and, having advanced near enough, for he is sure to measure the distance with accuracy, he flings his dart, and never fails to strike. The seal, terrified and wounded, dives in the greatest flurry; but a float being attached to the dart by a leathern line, he is soon forced up again, and is shortly despatched. They are then careful to stanch the wounds, to save as much of the blood as possible, and to distend the body, by blowing into the cellular part, as butchers sometimes are used to do, in order to make the body of the animal buoyant, otherwise it would go to the bottom as soon as dead.

Seal hunting, being their most profitable as well as most dangerous pursuit, is looked upon as the perfection of manly achievement. It forms the burden of praise to which every man aspires; and it is chiefly through the fame of having killed such a number of seals that any man can aim at pre-eminence. The unmarried women listen with eagerness when such great exploits are recounted; and a description of a seal hunt given, with proper emphasis and gesture, by the fortunate hunter, is sure to obtain general approbation. The applause which they bestow is not however clamorous, but tinctured with that decency and reserve for which they are remarkable. It is on such occasions that love matches usually are set on foot; and the successful candidate for the lady's hand must rely on the credit he has obtained by the number of seals he has taken.

There is very great danger to the Greenlander in the seal hunt. Should the seal be little exhausted in the chase, he often turns on his adversary, seizes on his kaiak, and with his sharp teeth pierces the flimsy cover, when no alternative remains to the poor Uskee but death, as his kaiak will sink and take him down. This must be certain; as the others can offer no assistance, except to allow him to hold by the end of another boat, to the great risk of him who navigates it. Except in the case of a father and son, such accommodation is very rare, as every man on such emergency naturally thinks of the value which his life is of to his own family. Much danger also is to be apprehended if the line get foul of the paddle, or arm, or even neck of the hunter, when the seal dives so suddenly on being wounded. It is then that the Uskee displays his skill and expertness. If upset, he raises himself again in his kaiak by a dexterous management of his paddle.

When assembled at a merry-making or at a marriage-feast, they are cheerful and joyous in the highest degree; but none of that boisterous rejoicing, which is considered the test of enjoyment in other places, is here known. The dance is practised in lively and tolerably well-executed movement; and some of the Danes having introduced the fiddle amongst them, they contrive to make out a pleasing entertainment. The men talk over their exploits in seal hunting, at which the boys are always attentive and silent hearers. Sometimes the song is raised, when one who leads the chorus repeats a line, and this is immediately succeeded by all the rest joining in a short accompaniment of no particular meaning.

They are extremely hospitable, particularly to any of their own nation who happen to pass near their abode, in removing from one place to another in search of seals. A brotherly invitation is instantly given, and the utmost attention paid to the stranger, who freely imparts his experience of the season, and receives in return such information as he requires. It is this interchange of good offices which makes them set so high a value on each other.

The language of the Greenlanders or Uskee-mès is very guttural. Like the Norwegians, they pronounce the letter *r* in the throat, so that it is not easy to distinguish many of their tones. They pronounce their words with great fluency; and their accents seem to be numerous, by the peculiar stress with which they deliver certain sounds. There are many consonants which they never use at the beginning of words, as they prefer commencing generally with a vowel. Even such words of other languages as they are desired to repeat, they dress in their own sounds; and if it begin with any of the proscribed letters, such is usually omitted, as was observed on the term Skrælling, which they converted into Karalit. They have no writing amongst them; though some of the children of the Danish convicts have been taught to write. The Uskees think it so much time thrown away from the more important concern of learning the management of the kaiak and dart. They usually reckon on their fingers, and seldom go beyond ten in counting; though others say they have been known to reckon as high as twenty. Their conveniences of life being so few, make further numbering unnecessary.

The following brief list of words from the language of the Greenlander is very insufficient to give any adequate idea of its construction; but, as it may aid further endeavours on such a subject, I beg leave to subjoin them, with their English signification.

Uskee . . . . The national denomination, to which is added me; and to this compound is attached the most honourable consideration.

Yak . . . . The national name so pronounced is insulting.

Cunà . . . . Woman.

Picanínnee	Child. A familiar diminutive generally applied.
Ap	Yes; probably an imitation of ay.
Na-me	Absolute refusal.
O-mu-as-a-wak ..	Will you go on board the ship?
Kai-n-u-kà	Affirmative reply to the former question.
Maize-wak	A ship.
Nella-nuc-a-tuck .	A watch.
Apleet	A gun.
Apatik.	Gloves.
Brumik	Bread.
Sucanuk	The sun.
Sucanungà	Greenland.
Tu-tu.........	A Deer.
Tri-u-ni-ak.....	A fox. The isatis of some writers.
Mikee	Dog.
Nannok	Bear.
Kazee	Ice.
Nunà	Yonder.
Manà	Land.
Pumà	Whale.
Pusee	Seal.
Sovitch	Knife.
Canu.........	Boat.
Kaiak	Boat.

CHAPTER IV.

OF THE ARCTIC ICE.

The stores of ice met with in high northern latitudes have naturally given rise to an idea, that the farther north the navigator proceeds, the more obstruction has he reason to apprehend from the presence of that body. Recent observations, and the experience of many years, have helped to remove that delusion. Wherever an extensive sea or ocean to the northward has been met with, the less has ice been found to prevail, and it is only in confined waters, such as are bounded by approximate lands, that heavy or thick ice is seen.

Experience has proved that the freezing takes place thus. In the shore of some island or large promontory, where the rock is present in great substance, if the wind be favourable to the change, the surface of the sea forms into small irregular cakes, generally hexagonal, interspersed with others of smaller size and similar form;* and if the congelation continue, these soon coalesce, and form a surface very little diversified; and after some time the icy mass extends itself, mostly towards the wind, then blowing, thicken-

* It is worthy of remark, that when a vessel sails in among this ice, as noticed in the Journal, the wind instantly falls nearly to a calm.

ing and spreading thus, until, a time incredibly short, a field of ice is formed leagues in extent, perfectly flat and even. Snow afterwards falling gives this ice a firmer consistence; and as any partial thaw of the snow may afterwards take place, the dissolved liquid, having no way of flowing off, lodges on the surface of the field, and congeals. By this process, in the course of the winter, all the inlets, straits, and narrow bays are chained together by a common tie. The first formation of the ice is called young ice.

It sometimes happens that the winds or currents not coming to act on some portions of the field ice, which is the name of it when properly and extensively formed, the vast tract may remain stationary in the place where it was originally formed, and continue to increase in thickness for more than one winter, as has been known to happen in the Waygat Sound, so as to be of a depth of from five to ten fathoms, when the tide or thaw has forced it from its lodgment. This ice is usually of saltish taste; but trial to that effect is mostly made upon pieces that have been rendered porous, or, as the sailors call them, rotten, from the increased temperature of the seawater.

When one of these fields of ice appears in the horizon a peculiar brightness is observed to be reflected on the air; and as there is generally present some vapour above the ice, the brightness is somewhat of a yellow tinge. A strong wind blowing over one of those fields of ice, which are usually, if not always covered with snow, the frozen snow is drifted along the clouds, and is peculiarly annoying, both from the increased cold and the sharpness of the particles.

The sailors call those drifts the barbers, from the effects produced by them upon the face. Mr. Ellis represents this drift of snow in Hudson's Bay, coming with a northwesterly wind, excessively keen, as small as grains of sand.

On the approach of spring, the winds, becoming violent, stir the sea very much, and this field ice then breaks up, and being carried forward, the pieces, crushing against each other, produce smaller ones, until the greater part is reduced to inconsiderable fragments; and these again, by the violence of succeeding winds, and the tossing of the waves, are heaped rudely on each other, and form what seamen call a pack of ice. The pack afterwards separating, the force of current, or some point of land, perhaps, breaks the aggregation into a less extensive and scattered train, which is then called a stream of ice. The packed ice is most dangerous to ships; for, if a vessel have the misfortune to be involved in such a situation, and it come to blow severely, the whole weight of this body presses against her sides; and instances have been known wherein a ship so circumstanced has been crushed like an egg-shell: or should her timbers be able to resist the terrible force of these fragments, they will continue to pile over one another like rocks, and finally either break or overwhelm the vessel by their weight. In such case, all hands must quit her, and provide for their safety as well as they can.

Another kind of ice remains for observation, in many respects differing from the former, and which has long engaged the attention of the naturalist: that is, the ice berg. From chemical experiments, it is well known that the freezing process approximates to that of boiling in its effects. The result in both is nearly alike. For instance, seawater boiled evaporates nearly free from the salts which it is known to contain in combination. If the vapour so raised be condensed, the quantity of water free from salt is nearly two thirds of the whole. Repeated distillations will make the product more pure; but this proportion rudely taken is tolerably near the truth. Now it is known also, by those who have had an opportunity of ascertaining the fact, that about two thirds of the substance of the ice berg is fresh water. Ships going into the Greenland seas and Davis's Straits in pursuit of the whale, are accustomed to have on board only a supply of water for the voyage out, as they are sure to have an abundance for consumption, both when on station there, and on return from the ice bergs, or, as they are called, islands of ice.

Frequently on those immense masses, which are sometimes more than a mile in extent, there are found large lakes of fresh waters formed by the action of the sun upon their summits, and from the snow with which they are generally covered. On days, when the state of the atmosphere is favourable to evaporation, these bergs are capped with a little fog, like a mountain peak. Sometimes the evaporation is so great as to envelope the ice island altogether, and render it invisible, at which time it is certain destruction for a ship to come to windward of it; for the tremendous chance is that she may come foul of it, a fate infinitely worse than were the vessel to encounter a rock. Unless a favourable wind, or the providential set of tide, aid in moving her from this formidable associate, the ship is in immediate danger of being buried beneath the ruins of the icy mountain, which are constantly tumbling from a height above the elevation of the mast, or the constant indraught against its sharp edges dashes her to pieces. In this awful emergency the men are active in taking to their boats without consideration of any thing but to save their lives. One half the vessels that are every year lost in the fisheries are owing to accidents of this kind, whence it is one of the great concerns of the watch upon deck to look out sharply for fear of falling in with an ice berg.

The numerous opinions hitherto advanced on the origin of those stupendous masses of congelation, have been advanced by persons who never had an opportunity of seeing the place whence they come. They are usually seen surrounded by field ice, when out at sea, that is, out of sight of land. They are also found frequently imbedded in field ice, near the land in the bays and fiords, (p. fiors, creeks,) where they are often grounded on the rocks. A ridge of submarine mountains, running across the straits from Reef Koll to the American land, is another theatre wherein they are arrested. The peaks beneath, at times surrounded with streams of ice, resemble an extensive city, with its towers, churches and monuments. North of Disko and of North-east Bay there is a deep recess, to the southward of Black Hook, where the tide stream forces in a vast number of ice islands, so much that the place is by seamen called Bergy Bay. Some ice bergs retain their situation a great length of time in particular places, and are recognised year after year by the whale hunters.

It would be an endless task to enumerate the variety of their forms; some peaked like a mountain; others with high, flat, table summits; and many with Gothic arches in them, frequently quite through, and of more than 100 feet in height. A violent wind often upsets such as become topheavy from the waves lessening their bulk below. One particular form of berg is most deserving of notice, and that is at present to be seen in Marshal's Bay, which lies to the northward of the Frow, or Women's Islands. There are two remarkable bergs of the description which sailors call ragged bergs. One of these is at least two miles in circumference, and its upper part is turreted with irregular square pillars at short intervals from each other, and with flat tops. These pillars have a basaltic shape in the fancy of an observer, and form the remarkable character of this kind of berg. The pillars are about thirty feet in height; and the base on which they stand is at least 100 feet above the surface of the sea, and has the appearance of being rent from some larger mass with great violence. There are numerous other immense bergs in the same bay, but this is the most remarkable.

Among the many names of respectable authority mentioned, as having offered an opinion with regard to the formation of the ice bergs, is that of Capt. Middleton. He accounts for them by supposing them as originally formed in the inlets or firths of Greenland, whence they are carried by a deluge or land flood, which breaks them loose, and forces them into the open sea, rather increasing than diminishing in bulk, where they continue floating about, until, after a lapse of some hundreds of years, they finally become dissolved between the fiftieth and fortieth degrees. Capt. Middleton further states that this deluge, or land flood, occurs about a regular period of seven years. Egede also asserts from his own knowledge, that the ice bergs are pieces of the ice mountains on the land, whence they are torn by land floods, and carried out to sea.

Now, as to Capt. Middleton's opinion, the account of the periodical deluge will to some appear rather apocryphal; and as to the bergs being formed in the inlets and firths, it is equally doubtful, as they are either forced into those situations by the stream of tide externally from north and north-west; or are driven down from the internal seas in the northern parts of Greenland, into some of those numerous firths, or rather straits, where their enormous bulk frequently causes an obstruction to the current, until the waters increase to such power as to drive every thing before them. Capt. Middleton's second assertion also is not supported by fact, as these ice bergs are constantly moving southward to be dissolved, are in continual diminution, and few of the immense numbers annually seen are recognised in the succeeding years, the whole of those that pass the latitude of Reef Koll regularly undergoing dissolution.

The opinion of Egede is probably accurate, so far as he has been an eyewitness. It is likely that the ice mountains which he saw, and which were stained brown by contact with rocks, induced him to conclude that they must have descended from high situations on the land. This, however, may rather be explained by these bergs having received the brown tinge, by striking against rocks, or jutting points of land, in their passage into the sea, from the original place in which they had been formed. Mr. Ellis states, that no ice mountains were to be seen in Repulse Bay, which is in the bottom of Hudson's Bay.

Had any of those gentlemen been so high as the seventy-seventh or seventy-eighth degree of latitude in Davis's Straits, they would have an easy means of accounting for this phenomenon. In the view of the extensive chain of islands (to which I have presumed to give the name of the Linnæan Isles) which stretch across the straits east and west, very nearly in a circular curve, as far as the power of vision can ascertain, there lies an immense continent of ice, rising towards the pole, and towards the islands before mentioned, descending like the regular declivity of the land mentioned by Bruce in the approach to the sources of the Nile. In this descent innumerable channels are visible, eaten away by the snow which is dissolved annually under the presence of the sun. In some places it out-tops the islands, but leans upon them all; and it is probably owing to this very chain of islands presenting an impenetrable barrier, that the descent of larger portions of the icy continent have not before now carried their chilling aspect into southern climates.

There can be, therefore, in my humble opinion, no doubt on the subject as to the original situation of the ice bergs. During the presence of a perpetual sun, the influence of that luminary is exercised with extraordinary force upon the icy continent, and causes those immense masses to be rent asunder from the continent, whence they are precipitated into the sea, and commence their progress to the southward. Carried thither by the tide stream, and under the force of a strong wind, they move along usually at the rate of two miles an hour, sometimes impelling before them fields of ice whole leagues in extent. I have myself heard the reports of these terrible disruptions, and the noise was as loud as thunder. In their way to the southward these bergs break with similar report, and finally fall into small pieces, and form streams of ice, which the sailors distinguish by their glassy blue colour to contain fresh water, and from them often collect a quantity for supply. Many of the bergs are traversed by blue veins, which are chasms filled with congealed snow water.

The ragged bergs so particularly noticed are good proof of what is above stated, as they are evidently a portion of the lower part of the continent, which had been channelled by the dissolved snow as stated. The columnar summits are nothing more than those parts which stood between the streams. Such as are aground, or have been so on rocks, are easily known by having a regular tide mark on them, and, for fear of latent danger, they are to be avoided. The ice bergs met in Hudson's Straits and Bays descend from the ice continent above the Linnæan Isles. Those met with in the Atlantic come from Spitzbergen.

CHAPTER V.

ARCTIC ZOOLOGY.

The subjects of zoology that came under observation in the northern seas, particularly in Davis's Strait, were pretty numerous. The main object of the voyage for which the ship had been sent out, being the pursuit of the whale, gave continual opportunities of traversing the latter sea in many directions, and consequently of seeing most of the animals, those especially of the larger sorts, which are there to be met with. The favourable state of the season, moreover, and the prevalence of north-easterly winds at an early part of the spring, produced unusually solvent effects on the field ice, so that the increasing power of the sun's heat caused it to break up much sooner than had been known for many years before, by which means the ships had access to higher latitudes than they had been ever known to reach at any former period. The arrangement of such animals as I have seen is conformable to the system of Linnæus, according to the last edition of his celebrated work by Gmelin.

Trichechus Rosmarus (the morse.) This clumsy and ferocious animal is rarely met with on the western shores of Greenland: his favourite haunts are on the side of Hudson's Bay, and the Island of Resolution.

In the latter place they are seen in great numbers; but being gregarious, and accustomed to come to each other's assistance when attacked, they are seldom hunted. Its tusks are considered very valuable, being of firmer consistence, and a better and more permanent white than ivory. The oil of the morse is much esteemed for its purity. The hide is convertible to many useful purposes, particularly on board the whale ships, where it is employed to prevent the masts, &c. from chafing. The usual food of the morse is seaweeds, corallines, and shell-fish. It is not carnivorous.

Phoca (the seal.) A great many species of this animal are met with along the western coast of Greenland. The most remarkable for numbers and frequency are the P. vitulina, or seacalf; P. Grænlandica, or harp-seal; P. hispida, or rough-seal; P. cristata, or crested seal; and P. barbata, or great-seal. Of these the first is most numerous, and is the chief wealth of the Greenlander. Every part of the animal is converted to some useful purpose. The skin serves for clothes, and is applied to the covering of the boats and tents, and it serves also for beds. The fat is the chief luxury of the Greenlander's habitation; and the tendons supply the place of thread, being easily separated into very fine fibres, and not at all injured by water.

The phoca vitulina, like the other animals of its kind, is gregarious, or rather they live in families, the old male being attended by his progeny for several generations. The teeth are very sharp, and the animal bites terribly, sometimes to the destruction of the poor Greenlander, as has been mentioned already. The habits of the seal are filthy, and singularly mischievous. A perpetual tyrant over weaker animals, he is also an object of constant pursuit with others. The white bear is constantly on the watch to surprise the seal when sleeping on the ice; but the latter has generally safe resources, taking possession of a single piece of ice from which he may command a good view of all around, and so that the proximity to the water may afford a ready escape. Sometimes they contrive to make holes in the field ice, through which they crawl, and never venture far from that situation for fear of being surprised by the bear or the Uskee-mè. They are easily stunned by a stroke on the forehead; but from this state they often recover; and, if not immediately despatched, are desperate in their revenge. The phoca vitulina, from constitution, is subject to the most violent impulses of anger, and nothing can withstand his rage when provoked. I have seen one of them after being hoisted on board, from the boat in which it had been carried apparently dead, from the blows inflicted on its head upon the ice, unexpectedly recover, and, seizing in its teeth the nearest object within reach, tear away such a portion as it could grasp. Even after death this irritation is strikingly manifest, as the muscular parts of the animal, though stripped of the external integuments, still retain the principle of vitality, and continue starting and quivering long after dismemberment of the body has taken place. Distinct portions of the flesh exhibit similar appearances; and it has often occurred that when under the hasty process of taking off the seal's skin and blubber, and although the animal has previously bled in profusion, as it would seem to exhaustion, yet in that mutilated state it has been seen, when heaved overboard, to swim off with vivacity. These seals are in best condition in May and June; but in the succeeding months they become quite lean and shy, and they are then seldom looked after for the sake of their fat. Seal oil is considered much more valuable than the whale oil, and is carefully kept apart for particular purposes. The greatest numbers are killed annually at the Spitzbergen fishery, and in that part of Davis's Strait which is known by the name of the South-west Country, about the sixty-fourth degree of latitude.

In the higher latitudes to the north-westward of Disko, the phoca barbata is mostly found; and they are usually of a great size, many of more than twelve feet in length, and of proportionate magnitude of body; but from the persecutions of the natives, and the advanced season when the ships get so far, very few of these are killed. This seal migrates in families, the elder ones leading the van, whilst the younger progeny follow confusedly behind, playing a thousand awkward tricks, tumbling and frisking along in the highest glee, and often in the extravagance of their fun flinging themselves quite out of the water. The sailors give to such assemblages the humorous name of "seals' weddings." The chief line of migration which they appear to move on is westward, and the groups which I observed invariably went in that direction.

Canis Familiaris (the dog.)—This useful and faithful animal is peculiarly valuable to the Greenlander, serving him in the capacity of a horse to draw his sledge over the snow, which he does with astonishing obedience. For this purpose, they are commonly yoked in pairs, and twelve are the usual number employed. The harness is nothing but light thong made of seal or deer-skin. The figure of the Greenland dog is singular. Of a size between the wolf and fox, he seems to partake of the appearance of both, but mostly resembles the latter. The snout is pointed; the ears short and erect; the tail is bushy and pendulous, but a little recurved; the body is covered with long rough hair, which is always erect, so as to give the animal in appearance a much larger size than natural; and the feet are small and neat. It is said to be little accustomed to bark, even in the chase. In times of scarcity, this faithful creature serves for food to his master, and its skin, from its long warm fur, affords comfortable clothing. It is chiefly made into caps, to be trafficked with the whale hunters every summer. The colour is variable, mostly black or gray.

Canis Lagopus (the arctic fox.)—This animal differs considerably from the common fox, and scarcely deserves that name. It is very variable in its colour at different seasons, being in winter found generally white, and in summer it exhibits a bluish tinge. The tail is straight and bushy, and the feet very much covered with hair; it is from the latter circumstance the animal takes its specific distinction. It is seen rarely in high situations, being chiefly near the shores, where it preys upon the ptarmigan, ducks, and smaller birds, and sometimes even on berries and shell-fish. It barks like a fox, but has not the disagreeable fetor of that animal. It assimilates also to the latter in being observed to burrow where the earth is favourable to such an operation. It is rarely met with in Greenland, on account of its being constantly hunted for the sake of its very valuable fur.

Ursus Maritimus, (the polar bear,) called also the white bear, and Greenland bear, from the situation in which it is usually found. The polar bear is generally enough known to make a description unnecessary. Its appearance is clumsy and awkward. The shuffling manner in which it moves would make one suppose its motion very slow, yet its speed is considerable. It is impatient of heat, and seems to have no other residence than the ice, on which it is found at immense distances from land; but as it derives all its sustenance from the sea, such as fish, seals, dead whales, and the minor cetaceous animals, that is its proper situation. The battles between the polar bear and morse are truly terrible; but the seal, P. vitulina, is by no means a match for such an adversary, and his only security is flight. The aspect of the bear is horrid, from his eye being covered with a nictitant membrane, similar to that with which the eyes of birds are provided. This membrane is highly useful to the animal, by sheathing his eye, and protecting the sight from the strong glare of the snow. His power of smelling is very great; and the sailors take advantage of this faculty to entice him within their reach, by burning a herring, the smell of which never fails to attract the animal.

When attacked, he rears himself erect on his hinder feet, and exposes his breast unknowingly to the danger, when the deadly spear is easily buried in his vitals. Instances have occurred when the savage animal, feeling the effects of the lance, has drawn it forth again with his paw and made his escape. If a female, and accompanied by her young, she will never forsake them, though ever so badly wounded; but, unmindful of her own safety, will use every exertion for the preservation of her cubs. The female is gravid from six to seven months, and brings forth two. It is a very rare occurrence to see two old bears in company; they are seen mostly solitary, or the female and her young ones. When looking out for prey they stand erect on their hinder feet, which gives them a more extensive prospect over the ice. They swim with great facility and force, and by this means pass from one field of ice to another. They can make very little resistance when attacked in the water, unless they can lay hold of the boat's gunwale with their paws, to prevent which the sailors often chop them off.

Monodon Monoceros, (the narval, or sea unicorn.)—It is mostly in very high latitudes, about the seventy-fifth degree and upwards, that this animal is found. Its horn, as it is called, is valuable, being considered excellent ivory. This tooth, properly so called, issues from the fore part of the upper jaw, just above the mouth. There are always two of these teeth, but one only attains the full growth, the matter of the smaller being absorbed during the increase of the larger: hence the name of the animal appears badly assigned. Diodon would evidently be more appropriate. The males alone are furnished with this formidable weapon; the females being destitute of it. The monodon is a beautiful animal. The skin is white, and elegantly mottled on the back and sides with black; the fins and tail are black. Like the whale, balæna mysticetus, in general structure, its habits are friendly to that animal; and they are frequently seen associated together. Their food is similar; and the only distinction from the character of its enormous companion, as to habits, is that the monodon is gregarious. The usual size of the monodon is fourteen feet, and sometimes a little more; and the tooth or horn is of an average length of seven feet. The mouth is very small; its greatest expansion being not more than six inches. The tongue is very short, immoveable, and placed very far behind. The passage to the stomach is very small, not three inches over.

When a number of these animals are together, they divert themselves in playing, when, their teeth appearing above the water, as if brandished about, have a singular effect; and the clattering noise they produce in this confused gamboling, would lead an inattentive spectator to suppose that some hostile proceeding was going forward, which is by no means the case. This has reference to the pacific habits of the monodon; but certainly such an extraordinary provision of annoyance could not have been dispensed for ornament sake; and though the creature being destitute of teeth in the mouth, and subsisting on mollusca and marine vegetables, seems little calculated for destructive or predatory life; yet this tremendous weapon must render him formidable to every inhabitant of the deep that obtrudes upon his peaceful haunts.

It has been said that the monodon attacks the

whale. No doubt such a conflict occasionally comes under observation; but it is not the simple, harmless, friendly, black whale, that becomes the object of retribution for injury received. Such tremendous retaliation is most frequently inflicted on the balæna physalus, the finner, whose depredations are indiscriminately exercised on every living creature that is inferior in muscular power; and few else exist in those regions, and in that medium in which animals of this order exercise peculiar dominion. The astonishing force with which the monodon urges his speed may be conceived from the fact of his tooth having been sometimes found driven through the planking of vessels navigating the Atlantic Ocean; the animal, in his fury, doubtless mistaking the body of the vessel for that of his adversary. In such an onset, the tooth is often snapped across, and is left in the wood through which it penetrated.

The monodon uses this instrument for the purpose of digging the sea plants from the rocks at great depths, not alone for the purpose of obtaining tender esculents, but with the intent of driving from their retreats the shrimps, mollusca, vermes, and other minute animals that constitute his peculiar food. The spiracles in his crown are double; but in their exit from the skin they unite and form a single aperture, through which the animal respires in a short and scarcely perceptible gust. His motion, when struck by a harpoon, is extremely confused. Seldom descending much below the surface of the water, he is easily taken; and a few thrusts of the whale lance are sufficient to effect the capture. The Greenland-men save nothing of the monodon but the blubber and tooth. The fins and tail being small, are not looked upon as of sufficient value to compensate the trouble of keeping.

Balæna Mysticetus, (the common whale.) This huge tenant of the sea is the chief object of the Greenland fishery: and for capture of this animal an expensive fleet is annually fitted out under the protection of the British Government. No name in zoology has been more preposterously applied than that of "fish," as generally including the balæna. The endeavours of Linnæus to establish a classification of animals on the principle of teeth being an organic distinction, expressive of the natural means of prolonging existence, is justly the admiration of every one who makes this branch of natural history a study. The energy of mind, precision, and copious brevity of that inimitable master, have done wonders for the advancement of science; and, like Bacon, he has added more to the mass of useful knowledge than all the cloud of dogmatists and logicians that for centuries has overshadowed the human mind.

In animals of the cetaceous order, however, the usual arrangement by the teeth, was in the Linnæan system necessarily abandoned, the distinctions, as insisted on by that great author, being inadequate to generic character; in place of which the following is given.

ORDER VII. *Cete.*—Spiracles situate in the crown, feet none, pectoral fins without nails, tail horizontal.

This description is liable to some objection, though, in general, sufficiently accurate to distinguish animals of this order from every other. They are all inhabitants of the sea; and all have a peculiar organization of body, by which they are an intermediate link between quadrupeds and fishes. Their bony framework is nearly similar in composition to that of the former, and it exhibits almost the same appearances when dry. The necessity of inhaling atmospheric air, with its effects on their blood, is also another point of comparison in which they closely approximate, whilst they bear resemblance to fishes in their long, tapering figure, calculated to make a speedy passage in the water. Destitute of hinder feet, they fall away remarkably from the previous orders of mammalia; but the spine, as in those animals, runs the full length of the body, terminating only in the angle where the portions of the tail divide. The tail is distinct from that of fish, being unfurnished with bone; being formed of a combination of cartilaginous, tendinous, and fatty substance; and being placed horizontally. Different from fishes also, animals of the cetaceous order are provided with instruments similar to fins, but of bony construction, much resembling the fore leg of quadrupeds, which to them supplies the use of the pectoral fin of fish, and of the fore arm of animals accustomed to grasp familiar or hostile objects. A stronger resemblance to fish is observable in others, having a dorsal fin; but when this comes to be examined, it is found to be an elevation of spinous processes with the common integuments, and not moveable in the manner in which fishes employ that appendage. Cetaceous animals possessed of the dorsal fin are usually hostile to those destitute of it; and those furnished with teeth are very remarkable for predaceous character. Like quadrupeds they are all viviparous; and from their habit of suckling their offspring, are properly classed with the mammalia.

The head of the balæna mysticetus is about one third of the length of the body, but often exceeds that dimension. The remaining two thirds are evenly divided by the parts of generation. In the female the pudendum is situated between the mamillary vessels, which are closely adjoining, in a parallel line; the vent being situated at a short distance below. A long groove up the belly of the male serves as a lodgment for the penis; the testes being concealed beneath the integuments, and not obvious to view. The teats of the female are of strong cartilaginous substance; and when drawn beyond the skin, are about three inches in length. When suckling her young, which is most commonly an individual, the parent turns on her side, and has then the advantage of taking in a great view with the eye above water, when, if any danger is apprehended, she instantly descends, carrying off her young beneath her fin. If the young whale happen to be struck, the harpooner is sure of capturing the parent, as she never forsakes her offspring. The eye of the whale is scarcely larger than that of an ox, and is furnished with lids. The ear is scarcely perceptible, being a perforation not larger than the tube of a goose-quill.

The balæna mysticetus, or blubber whale, has received its specific name from the Scriptural record of the adventure of Jonas. Linnæus has left no explanation of many terms employed in this manner; and conjecture must, as on the present occasion, be employed in aid of discovery. Crantz has put his authority forward in opposition to that of the illustrious Swede, and states that the squalus car charias, white shark, was more likely to afford the necessary accommodation for the recreant prophet than the balæna: with the latter, however, one would suppose the man would have a better chance of escape.

Many species of whale are seen in the northern seas, a certain degree of cold seeming necessary to their habits. They are observed to traverse the western ocean as low as the fiftieth degree, but rarely below the fifty-fourth north latitude. Of such as frequent the seas about Spitzbergen, Davis's Strait and Hudson's Bay, the balæna mysticetus or common black whale, B. physalus or finner, B. boops or pike-headed whale, and B. musculus or broad-nosed whale, are the most remarkable. Indeed, the distinctions of the two latter species from the finner are so indefinite, and the animals are so seldom seen, that it may be supposed, with little injury to accurate description, that they are only varieties of the same species. They shall however be mentioned separately according to the arrangement in the system.

The blubber whale being an object of more decided distinction, on account of the avidity with which it is pursued for the sake of its commercial produce, is deservedly placed foremost as a subject of natural curiosity, after the diodon* has been exhibited. Anomalous of the generation of quadrupeds, though similarly

* Monodon.

propagated, and differing essentially from the finny class, in whose peculiar medium they exist, and if possible, farther removed from the amphibious animals than from the two former, the whales of this specific denomination are in characteristics widely removed from the ordinary classification of animals. The most obvious notice, which a naturalist would take of this enormous animal, would embrace its timidity, and its immense volume of body, indicating at the same time resistless strength. Seldom, when adult, under the dimension of sixty feet in length, sometimes attaining a size half as great again, and moving in a medium peculiarly suited to his form, the whale must be possessed of tremendous power; and his efforts under the influence of fear or anger are truly awful, when man, as observer of those efforts, compares his might and volume with such enlarged examples of muscular power.

One remarkable distinction in these animals, which, as it marks a good anatomical criterion, and has not hitherto, so far as within my knowledge, been made public, is that whales seem to possess an extraordinary provision of arterial blood. The remark applies also to seals, and almost all the animals, particularly of the cetaceous order, in cold climates. The Uskee-mè, even, is oppressed by an overflow of that vital current, when the heat of summer forces a more rapid circulation. All those subsisting on assimilated food, and subjected nearly to similar temperature, approximate surprisingly in constitution. The Greenlander bleeds profusely from the nose, if no accident afford the salutary evacuation in any other mode, during the active and dangerous season of the summer; nor does he consider the loss of blood on such occasions an injury. Wound a seal about the same time, that is, before he becomes exhausted by the natural occupations of the season, and the profusion of arterial blood is astonishing for the size of the animal. The whale is an extraordinary proof of the accumulation which this portion of vital matter may attain in an animal's frame.

Early writers on natural history have drawn conclusions as to the prolongation of life, which they would represent as indispensable in circulation of the blood. If an animal, according to such opinion, is obliged to live in water, and occasionally to respire atmospheric air, some peculiar organization of the heart becomes a necessary means of explaining the phenomenon. What may be the proper agency of the heart in the circulation of the blood, most probably will long remain to be explained. This is applied to the received opinion that a passage in the heart, called the foramen ovale, is essential to the continuation of life in such animals as dive long and frequently under the surface of water. The seal is made a memorable instance of this necessary conformation of that viscus as connected with the existing wants of that animal. The opportunities afforded me, however, of examining the structure of the seal's heart were far from convincing that the foramen ovale existed in the seal. The best investigator may be mistaken from appearances; but where the eye, as well as the touch, is applied in evidence, and the alleged circumstance is not found, it may be pronounced hardihood to bear out the story by assertion. I have anxiously tried to ascertain the existence of such a passage between the chambers of the vital reservoir in the animal now mentioned, but was in no instance able to trace any such permeation.

Now, instead of looking to this accidental passage in the heart as essential to the continuation of life in animals that seek their sustenance in water, a more obvious resource may be resorted to as explaining this phenomenon; and no division of animals presents this in better form than the cetaceous, both from the magnitude of the scale, and their peculiar habits. The extraordinary degree of warmth, which is evident in the constitution of these animals, seems at once to prove the existence of great abundance of arterial fluid, which is the proper source of animal heat. In the monodon, and B. mysticetus, this is strongly evidenced; the spinal canal containing scarcely any of the substance called medullary, and the jaw-bones, in their posterior foramina, being of immense size, and like the spinal canal, exhibiting a facia of blood-vessels of a calibre and abundance that would appear fully sufficient to supply the extraordinary heat above noticed.

What may be the functions of the lungs under such circumstances, whether different, in increase or diminution of action, from those of quadrupeds constantly living in the medium of atmospheric air, is difficult to determine. Whales, as well as seals, sleep in such situations as afford a constant supply of air; the former on ice or rocks, and the latter at the surface of the sea. A circumstance, however, which I beg leave to mention, with an expression of little doubt as to the accuracy of the account, would appear to place in considerable difficulty an attempt at explaining the true action of the pulmonary organ in those animals when in a state of rest. I have been assured by a respectable master of a Davis's Strait whaler, that some few years since a native paddled alongside, making anxious expression of useful information which he had to communicate. It was, that he and his companions had, during three days, previously observed a large whale sleeping at the bottom in a neighbouring creek. On sending some boats to the spot, and splicing together some oars, by this means sending down a harpoon, the animal was struck, and subsequently taken. In such case, does the action of the lungs remain suspended? or does the arterial circulation proceed so as to supply sufficient vitality?

When the whale is struck, arterial blood flows profusely. When the progress of destruction advances far enough to require the exhausted animal to respire more frequently, he blows arterial blood mixed with water; and when the lance has been repeatedly plunged into his vitals, the column ascending from the blow holes (spiracles) is of a vivid red, compared as it has been, not unaptly, to the flame issuing from a furnace: but when the arterial current is exhausted, and the animal is nearly subdued, then the column assumes a darker hue; and as death is nearer, it becomes a deep brown purple, till with one immense effort of expiration the triumph is decided. At this signal the hunters raise the shout of death, and proceed to tow away their enormous captive.

This question narrows exceedingly, in ordinary view, if the chambers of the heart be considered decisive of the fact. Such an immense supply of arterial blood would require an enlarged cavity for its reception and further distribution; but here again a difficulty arises, with regard to the uses of such numerous blood-vessels as the spinal canal and the foramina of the bones of the head present. The examination of the whale's heart exhibits no deviation from the ordinary construction of that viscus in other mammalious animals. As it lives always in the water, it would require the transit of blood by the foramen ovale, much more than the seal, were such necessary; but no such opening exists. It therefore remains for anatomical research to account for the animal economy of the whale on other principles than those hitherto adduced.

The social haunts of the blubber whale appear to be confined to the inland waters of Greenland; which, being of unascertained depth and extent, and sheltering the timid and unoffending creature from the numerous enemies by which he is persecuted, is anxiously sought after, when the urgency of sexual appetite forces him not from this his peculiar home. This properly refers to such as inhabit the northern seas. How the animal is occupied during the winter months, whether sunk in perpetual slumber, which is probable, during that period, or more actively engaged in feeding on the mollusca, and such minute animals of the crustaceous class as form his accustomed food, and with which those confined and tranquil waters may be supposed to abound, cannot with any plausibility be ascertained. Yet when it is considered in what places the whale is first seen on the return of summer, and the direction in which it runs at that peculiar season, little doubt can be entertained of the retreats whence it has issued.

Voyagers to Hudson's Bay seldom see the "first regular whales," until about the sixty-third degree. In the southwest seas in Davis's Strait, they are in the early part of the season oftentimes killed in great numbers. Higher up the Strait, they are seldom seen till after passing Baal's River; and off South Bay, Western Islands, and in Disko, or South-East Bay, they become numerous, but are not stationary; in general running to the northward, to the north-eastward, or westward. Their haunts in such cases are far from regular, as what is deemed in one year successful fishing ground, becomes in succeeding summers quite otherwise. In this respect, no doubt, these animals are regulated by experience of such annoyance as they have met with previously.

On the eastern side of Greenland, towards Spitzbergen, they are seen in immense numbers about the 64th degree, but the majority are females attended by their young; whilst on the west side of Greenland the sexes are nearly equal in number, and few young ones are seen. Further westward, towards the shores of North America, males are more frequently seen than in the other places, and always of superior size; and in the high latitudes in West Greenland, above the Women's Islands, and throughout the wide fiords along the coast to Devil's Thumb and the Linnæan Isles, the largest whales are usually found. The latter seem to be their *ne plus ultra;* and of this I shall give satisfactory evidence.

The continual necessity this creature feels of respiring from the atmosphere drives him constantly to the surface. From his numerous pursuers, the field ice presents occasional retreat; and some of the mile-length bergs afford a similar security. As such retreats always meet the exigencies of the whale from the northward, it becomes habitual for him to move in that direction; and thither also his partner flies for protection of herself and young one, to obtain such concealment as the time requires; but having reached the places above mentioned, further flight is impracticable; the continual presence of ice affording no open water for breathing space, the continent of massy congelation being there unbroken except at its precipitous limits. The whales must in this case either return southward again, or move in an easterly or westerly direction. The purposes for which they have traversed nearly twenty degrees of the northern deep, and encountered the innumerable perils of the way, will not admit of premature return; and there they remain running, as the whale hunters well know, from the islands of West Greenland, into the untracked ocean towards America; and again returning, nearly in the same parallel, to the Greenland bays. Whether the animals following such contrary courses be the same, must of course remain doubtful; but that they do proceed in that direction, admits of not a shade of question.

It may be matter of entertainment to give a short view of the mode in which the whale is hunted. Every ship engaged in this branch of commerce, from British ports, is furnished with six boats, besides the ship's, or jolly-boat. One of these is called the gig-boat, or No. 1: the remaining five are distinguished only by their number. The gig is provided with six oars, besides the steersman's; the rest have only five oars each, with the same exception: in all, the harpooner uses the bow or foremost oar. Each boat is provided with three lines, of 120 fathoms each, made of the very soundest hemp; as on the faithfulness of the line the success of capture depends. These lines are coiled with great care and nicety in a square frame in the middle of the boat, and the harpooner has his weapon ready in a dry place, to set it on a rest prepared for that purpose on the right bow of the boat. The boat-steerer, who must be trained to his station, as in emergency his courage and caution may not only secure success but save the lives of the men, is provided with a long oar, with which he dexterously directs the motion of the boat. Each boat is also provided with a tin trumpet to announce the station or movement in case of being enveloped in fog; and also with a piece of bunting attached to a short pole by way of signal flag.

Thus equipped, the boats are suspended by a simple machinery of ropes and blocks by the ship's sides, ready to be lowered in an instant. To the mainmast is attached, at a great elevation, usually about 100 feet above the deck, a structure resembling a water cask, called a hurricane house, in which the master or confidential officer is stationed with a telescope on the look-out; and to such as have not witnessed the fatigues of that station, a recital of its dangerous hardships would appear incredible. In the sudden transitions from intense cold to the most annoying heat, whilst the head is involved in the blaze of an eternal unclouded sun, that blisters the face and blinds the strongest vision, that situation must be inflexibly maintained, and such perseverance often costs the individual the loss of health and life.

If the ship's station be on what is considered good fishing ground, which is commonly known from the water being of a deep olive colour, a boat or two being kept continually on the watch, the moment a whale is descried, the pursuit commences without loss of a second of time; and as the ordinary speed of the whale boats is six miles an hour, a very short space of time is sufficient to bring them to the spot. The whale, on the first rising, seeing no enemy near, and not apprehending danger, is apt to repose a considerable time at the surface, apparently "stretched out o'er many a rood," and the boats are meantime advancing to the place. "Give way" is then the word with which the rowers urge their speed, and the harpooner, with desperate and determined energy, buries his weapon in the animal's body. This is mostly followed by a moment's awful pause; the whale, upon feeling the smart of the barb, trembles for an instant in his posture, darts precipitately forward, or sinks by an unaccountable effort with the suddenness of so much lead. If the harpoon remain fast, the line continuing to run with immeasurable velocity, the flag of the boat is displayed in token of success, when all in the boats within sight of the transaction, and those on board the ship, join in a wild irregular cry of "A fall, a fall,"* and a flag is immediately run up to the mizzen mast head to proclaim the vessel's good fortune.

In the mean while the other boats are despatched to aid in the capture, and no sooner does the animal rise again, than the next harpooner secures him by a second wound, and so follow as many as they can, until by multiplied efforts to escape, compelled so repeatedly to rise for breath, and then almost instantly visited with the instruments of death, exhaustion follows, and he becomes a bestunned object for the hunter's deliberate aim, when, from the numberless plunges of the lance, the vital current becomes spent, and the animal dies. Such an event is not always unattended with danger to the hunters.

Often in the first instance of being stricken, if recollection of similar injury aid his anger, the retaliation of the animal is destructive, for, rushing backwards, in which direction the assailants usually advance, a single touch of the tail is sufficient for their destruction. The sudden violence with which the animal descends frequently produces a similar effect if the line happen to meet obstruction in its course; and in the dying scene, pierced with many wounds, the animal exhibits a terrific object by the mightiness of his efforts, though quite unconscious of the grand effects produced by such exertions. Spouting a column of apparent flame, which, descending, covers the sea with a crimsoned surface of acres in extent, at the same time lashing the water all around into purple

* The cry of "A fall, a fall," seems to be expressive of having taken a whale, the Dutch in their jargonous language giving it origin.

foam by the strokes of the fins and tail, now and then endeavouring to replunge in hopes of escaping, in which effort half the body towards the tail is seen above water, the danger so obvious is carefully avoided by the boats' crews, at that crisis cautioned to remain at a secure distance, when the lines fastened to the harpoons are slowly drawn in till the animal re-appears and breathes his last.

The whale, after death, always turns on the back. The fins are then lashed together, perforations are made in the tail, and a rope is passed through, and thence round the rump; when all the boats, passing lines from one to the other, proceed to tow the monster towards the ship, which is usually so managed as to meet them, in order to lessen the fatigue. When brought alongside, the body is properly secured for the operation of flinching. This consists in digging off the blubber, or cellular substance, from the muscular parts, in large slips, sometimes of half a ton weight, but all of a regular form, which are lifted on deck by the help of the windlass, and the labour of many hands, who toil incessantly until the spoliation is completed. The whale-bone, as it is called, is carefully dug out, as well as the massy tongue; the former for its peculiar importance, and the latter as being almost entirely of blubber. The bones of the lower jaw are also removed, being a private perquisite of the master, and so would the frontal or crown bone too, were it not for the extreme difficulty of separating it from the body. Then finally the remotest joint that can be marked in the lumbar vertebræ or rump, is severed, and the crang,* as is called the residue of the animal, with its abdominal contents, is suffered to sink, which it instantly does to the bottom.

When the flinched pieces are hoisted on deck, they are cut into squares, and tossed into the body of the vessel, where they remain for a convenient opportunity of reducing them to handbreadth slips, which is done by chopping them, upon portions of the tail, with heavy knives; and this procedure, which is called "making off," is final for the transmission of blubber to the English ports from the different fishing grounds. The reduced pieces are for that purpose placed in large casks, and closely bunged up to prevent the action of the air from producing the putrefactive process.

During the foregoing operations, the utmost precautions are observed that no portion of muscular flesh be mixed with the cellular part, as the violent explosion of the cask would be the consequence, when coming into southern climates. Similar concern is also evinced that the sawdust of the pine should not have admittance into the casks containing the blubber, from an experience that the casks in such case are more certainly burst by the evolution of gases in an earlier stage of putrefaction than even by the presence of the former. To prevent the first from taking effect, the muscular parts, and skin, are carefully cut away in the "making off;" and the sawdust is employed so cautiously, and in such small quantities, that no abuse of that dangerous material can be apprehended. The

* Crang probably bears some relation to the Latin term for muscular flesh.

chief reason why sawdust is employed, is for the purpose of drying up the oily effusions that incommode the men in the use of the respective implements necessary to effect the operations of flinching and making off. The use of fir-timber dust on such occasions cleanses the hands and instruments, with a ready and efficient result; and the ship boys are stationed so as to supply the demands of the officers in this respect.

The integuments of the whale are, like the animal himself, widely different from that of every other in comparison. The epidermis is like thin parchment, flexible when on the body, easily detached, wrinkled according to the age of the animal, and corresponding with the organization of the muscles beneath; but, when dry, it is horny and brittle, and in consistence similar to the finer laminæ of the whale-bone. The true skin is about an inch thick in its full character, and is formed of material analogous to the whale-bone, but breaks, when dry, in perpendicular fissure: it is usually a deep brownish black, and, when soft, strongly resembles Indian-rubber. In composition it seems to differ very little from the substance that constitutes the matricular bed of the whale-bone; the white colour of the latter forming the only distinction, except that its fracture is shelving. The cellular tissue, or blubber, is, in its average thickness, twelve inches; in the very young whale, being gelatinous; in the more advanced and vigorous, of a florid red, when it is considered most valuable; and in the aged animal, yellow and tough from the induration of increased and condensed fibre: for which reason the older whales are not so much an object, where choice presents, as those of less advanced growth.

The older ones are also more dangerous and difficult to take, both from the rigidity of their frame, and their experience of injury. It is not unusual when they happen to be disturbed in the pursuits that draw them from their retreats, that, if a partner be wounded, the affectionate companion comes to give relief, not knowing the cause of the pain, or of the sudden flight. In the search, the watchful hunter strikes the fresh prey, when the tortured animals, seeking each other in their anguish, and desperate with their wounds, often run foul of the boats, and involve their pursuers in the ruin that overwhelms themselves. In some instances, as heretofore observed, they, by running among packed ice, or rubbing the line against the edge of a flaw, (a portion of field ice,) frequently chafe it so as to make it snap, and so escape for the moment, but they are seldom eventually safe.* On such occasions they cease not to run for unknown length, until fatigue or death makes them insensible of pain. To some such occurrence is to be attributed the circumstance of a whale having been captured with the harpoon imbedded in its body, after traversing the unknown seas between Spitzbergen and Davis's Strait.

I cannot conclude this part of the subject without mentioning the singular character of courage and intrepidity evinced by the men employed in the capture

* "Hæret lateri lethalis arundo."

of the whale. Trained to the occupation from boyhood, and induced by rewards of much importance in their station, such qualifications are highly recommendatory in their application for employment; and, in their voyage, should "good luck" attend their exertions, and an implicit devotedness to the interests of the owner be evinced, their advancement and emolument are certain. The expense of outfit, the danger of total loss by shipwreck, and the thousand casualties to which this branch of trade is liable, should prevent all envy of the profits arising from it. When successful, these profits are certainly great; but they are fairly balanced, not only by the constant and straining anxiety attending selfish concern, but by the apprehension that all the individuals so engaged may probably never return from so perilous a mission. Such reflections consume an honest and humane heart; whilst the purse of the adventuring merchant may be distended by the fortunate return.* Indeed, under every consideration, few would be found to envy an adventure of such description. The legislature has placed ample protection over this trade, holding forth every encouragement to men of enterprise and capital to promote it. The late long war has also contributed to make it a sort of monopoly to the British merchant; but when the yearly diminution that at present exists has continued, whales in the northern seas will become as scarce as wolves in Britain.

Balæna Mysticetus (the finner) bears a great re-

* The whale averages a value of 1000*l*.

semblance to the former, in the generic character of the double spiracle on the crown, but differs from it in having, at the extremity of the dorsal vertebræ, a soft fin.

The finner is seen traversing the ocean between Newfoundland and the British islands, in numbers; but in the months in which the blubber whale sallies forth from his haunts, they are observed running towards the arctic seas, and are considered good guides to the whale's retreats. Like that animal, the place of teeth in the mouth is supplied by horny laminæ imbedded in the frontal bone; but in the finner, those laminæ are shorter, and of a blue colour, which, from whatever cause proceeding, renders it less fit for the impression of those colouring materials, by which the common whale-bone is adapted to so many useful and elegant purposes. The finner being also much thinner in blubber, of course more slender, though generally surpassing the blubber whale in length of body, is less the object of pursuit. Besides, the hunters from experience avoid striking the finner, well knowing his enormous strength and fleetness; always when wounded, running forwards with such velocity as to distance his pursuers in a few minutes, and frequently snapping the lines; or, should the harpooner hold fast, himself and the boat's crew would soon be out of reach of all reasonable assistance. Hence these animals are very seldom captured.

The finner is gregarious, being usually in herds of from five to a dozen; and they are, at any distance, easily distinguishable from the blubber whale by the strength, elevation, and whiteness of the watery column discharged from the blow-holes. The blast of the blubber whale is short, full, and brownish, driven somewhat forward; whilst that of the finner is forced directly upwards in a firm column of more than ten feet, and with such an accompanying gust as may be heard in a calm evening at the distance of more than half a mile. The attention of the sailors is drawn to the path of the finner by the noise of this discharge; and should the animal be then beneath the surface, and his course be marked by the eddying ripple caused by his motion like that of the blubber whale, on ascertaining the finner's blast, the preparations for pursuit are instantly suspended.

With regard to the balæna boops, or pike-headed whale, and the balæna musculus, or broad-nosed whale, I have already some reason to suppose they have the best place in a description on the page of a publication on natural history professedly directed to exhibit new species. They shall for that reason be included in the general description of the former species.

The physeter, or cachalot, is seldom caught in Davis's Strait, especially the P. macrocephalus or spermaceti whale. It is from the head of this animal that spermaceti is obtained; and from its intestines, when diseased, the substance of ambergrise is procured. Those seen in Davis's Strait are now very rare. The body is generally whitish and smooth. It has a double row of teeth in the lower jaw, forty-six in number, which are received into sockets in the upper.

The physeter microps, or sharp-nosed cachalot, is

sometimes, but very rarely, seen in the northern seas. I had an opportunity of observing only one in Davis's Strait.

Delphinus phocæna, or common porpoise, is frequently seen in numerous shoals in the Strait, tumbling about in the roughest waves as if in sport. The general length of this animal is seven feet. The usual food of the porpoise are herrings and small fish; but of these I never saw any in Davis's Strait.

Delphinus Orca, (common grampus.)—There are two varieties of this genus to be met with in the northern seas. They differ from the porpoise, in the snout of the former being not so blunt; whilst that of the grampus is short, blunt, and a little turned up. The remarkable difference of size too is very striking, the grampus being from twenty to twenty-four feet long, and proportionally bulky. The latter also is furnished only with forty teeth; whilst the former has forty-six in each jaw.

The second variety of D. orca, sword grampus, has the dorsal fin long and bony, broad at the base, and curved like a scymeter. As they advance in age, this instrument grows longer; so that the leader, or old one, can be distinguished from his followers by the superior height of the fin. This is one of the fiercest enemies of the whale, being provided with such an efficient weapon of annoyance as the strong dorsal fin. The sword grampus pursues also seals; and the latter, in their clumsy efforts to escape upon the ice or rocks, are frequently overtaken by their active adversary, when the seals are swept from their place of retreat back into the water, where they are easily vanquished.

The sword grampus varies much in size according to age; but when full grown, it is above twenty feet long. The great size of the fin, from which the animal derives its trivial name, distinguishes it among the dolphins as much as a similar instrument does the physeter turfio among the cachalots.

Delphinus Leucas, (white whale or beluga.)—Snout conic, obtuse, inclined upwards; dorsal fin wanting. This beautiful animal diversifies many a dreary scene in the arctic seas, where all animated existence would seem shut out by the eternal presence of ice, and its accompanying cold. When every wind is hushed, and the surface of the sea becomes of glassy smoothness, a lively herd of these gregarious animals, by their merry gambols, and the exhibition of their smooth, slippery white bodies, affords a pleasing and entertaining view. As in other cetaceous animals, their pectoral fins partake more of the character of the fore feet in quadrupeds than the pectoral fins of fishes, being constructed of fine bones, of a very porous kind, covered with a little fat, much cartilage, and a thick, tough skin, with an epidermis. The young are dusky, or mottled obscurely; but that distinction, I apprehend, is not decidedly accurate, as many of that dusky colour, which I have seen, were equal in size to their white companions, and some even surpassed them in magnitude. The teeth in the jaws of the white whale are short and bluntish, in number amounting to thirty-six. The usual size of the white whale, when full grown, is from twelve to fifteen feet, and not very bulky for that length. There is not, at a great distance, much difference between the D. leucas and the monodon, their movements being much alike.

Having laid before the reader this short and faithful account of the mammalious animals, I shall proceed to enumerate the various birds that came actually under my observation, and will briefly detail such of their habits as I had an opportunity of noticing myself, or of collecting from the accounts of persons, who, from many years' experience, have been eyewitnesses of those habits.

Corvus Corax (the raven) is not common in the arctic regions, though observed in very high latitudes. Seldom seen in pairs, this bird leads a solitary life, alternately frequenting the ice in the early part of the day, and returning to its rocky retreats in the afternoon. One remarkable circumstance regarding this bird, in Greenland, is the peculiarity of note which it utters when perched upon its craggy seat,—not that deep, hoarse, croaking that announces its ominous presence in Europe, but a shrill and rather pleasing, soft, short note, greatly resembling the barking of a dog, or such as the fox is heard to utter when in chase of his prey. On first hearing this note, I was much surprised, supposing it to come from the arctic fox, or other such quadruped; but the sudden presence of the raven descending from the lofty brow of Disko, and uttering this singular cry, put the circumstance beyond doubt. The Greenlanders eat the flesh of this bird, convert the skin into inner garments, and make fishing lines of the quills.

Anas Mollissima, (the eider duck.)—Male—bill, legs, front, ocular band, breast, rump and belly, black: crown, shoulders and wing coverts, white, with a green blotch on the nape. Female—almost wholly ferruginous, or rusty brown, with darker lines: tail and primary quill feathers, dusky. Length—22 inches. Food—testaceous animals. Eggs—five, greenish, with a tinge of brown, and larger than those of the tame duck, which, as well as the flesh of the bird, are excellent food when fresh. The nest is constructed of dry vegetables, and strewed over with the rich down of the bird, which is either shed from the heat of incubation, or is pulled off for the purpose of increasing the warmth. The plumage constitutes the valuable eider down.

The vast flocks of these birds, that annually visit the shores of Greenland for the purpose of rearing their young, are surprising to one unaccustomed to see animals so highly prized for their down. It would be needless to particularize any bay, inlet, or creek, as most remarkable for the retreat of these birds during the season of incubation; they are however careful to avoid the presence of the natives as much as possible; and they are generally found by the whale ships where Uskees are not seen. In Hickson's Bay, for instance, and in the fiords farther to the northward, they are seen in immense numbers, where boats may be laden with their eggs without difficulty, and a good marksman may easily possess himself of many of the birds themselves, as both male and female are not much alarmed at the presence of strangers who come so unexpectedly as the whale hunters do. The great concern of the season never allowing the ships to remain long in one station, unless impeded by the ice, or the whales appearing in great number, prevents the slaughter of the eider duck to the amount that would otherwise occur every year.

The masters of the whale ships are anxious to fetch home the skins of the eider ducks, as presents to their friends, when the coarser feathers are plucked off, and the skin stretched so as to be preserved dry with the down on; in which state they are considered highly salutary in application to the breasts of newly lain-in women. These skins form the great luxury of such of the natives of Greenland as can reserve them for their private use; but they are of too much value in the estimation of the Danes not to induce a barter of them for some iron nails, and other such important equivalents.

Anas Boschas (the common wild duck) is also very numerous.

Procellaria Glacialis, (fulmar petrel, or mallemuck.) —There are many varieties of this bird. If colour constitute specific distinctions, there are many species under this name. As this is one of the most remarkable birds that frequent the Straits during the Summer months, a particular description may be deemed necessary.

1. Head, breast and belly, white; back and wings, hoary; legs, yellowish; bill, pale ash, yellowish at the tip; nostrils, composed of two tubes lying along the bill, and lodged in one sheath.

2. Head, whitish; neck, back, wing and tail,

darker gray than the 1st; legs and bill corresponding.

3. Body and wings cinereous gray.

4. Body, wings and tail, almost brown, with a grayish tint.

The first three are properly called mallemuck, and the sailors give the name of spectioneer to the fourth, to which, from its singularly filthy and voracious habits, and also from a view of its enormous œsophagus, which extends the whole length of the body, the stomach being situate near the vent, the name specifically designating its qualities—gulosa, or gormandizing petrel, would be more appropriate. Besides, these birds are found all over the ocean, and visit the icy seas only in the summer months.

From their similarity of colour and size, they would at first view appear to be gulls; and some writers even describe them as such, wherever they happen to be met with at sea, particularly in fine weather; but this error is easily rectified, when one comes to examine the peculiar character of their tubular nostril, which is, to use a familiar phrase, like a double-barrelled pistol. In a heavy gale, the fulmar petrel is more readily distinguished by the strength and facility of his flight; like all the birds of that genus, seeming to take pleasure in the storm, with the greatest ease skimming in every direction with truly astonishing speed, playing round the ship when running ten knots an hour, and sometimes breasting the mountainous wave within half an inch of the surface, ascending to its greatest elevation, and in that manner following it as closely in its precipitous descent.

The ordinary length of the mallemuck is seventeen inches; the younger ones not so large. When old, they are easily known by their increased voracity, and the tyrannous disposition they manifest towards the younger and more timid. Stupid and fearless, they will approach near enough to be killed by the stroke of a boat-hook or oar, if tempted by a piece of blubber or other fat; and, after being stunned and taken into the boat, on recovering ever so little, if their favourite blubber be within reach, they will greedily swallow it; and it must be a very large piece that will not find its way down with them. As they appear in the northern seas, they seem to have, each, but an individual concern; so that the distinctions of sex cannot be determined from common observation. When sated, it is true, they compliment each other in a short chuckling note, like caw, caw; but this harmony is easily broken by casting among them a piece of blubber, too large to swallow, when they commence an angry contest for the prize, and the most courageous generally remains solitary at the feast. This envious and rapacious disposition affords the sailors an opportunity of amusing themselves, by tying two pieces of blubber to the ends of a string, when a ridiculous scene ensues; one end being swallowed by one mallemuck, the other is seized and perhaps gorged by another, and the prize is thus several times alternately hauled out of each other's throats.

The immense numbers of these birds that annually resort to Davis's Strait are surprising. Their probable breeding haunts must be somewhere in the southern shores of Greenland, or on the coasts about

Hudson's Strait; for it is after coming into those latitudes that they are observed to increase most in number. They are of importance to the whale hunters, showing by their flight the retreats of that animal; and this indication is always relied on and followed. The mallemuck possesses the sense of smelling in a very acute degree; for if at any time not one of these birds is to be seen, a small bit of blubber thrown overboard will attract them immediately in great numbers.

Procellaria Gravis, (the cape hen.) This familiar name is given by the sailors to *a new species* of petrel, seen only in the latitude of Cape Farewell and Staten Hook, and somewhat farther eastward during the summer months; frequenting Newfoundland in the latter season. Bill and legs, black; nostrils, tubular; throat, breast, and belly, white; crown, nape, back, and wings, sooty brown; tail, brown, with a white band across; ends of the quill-feathers, touched with white; band on the eyes, black; wings, very long.

The usual length of this bird is nineteen inches; and, like the others of the genus, it can exert amazing velocity; seldom striking downwards with the wing, particularly in a strong wind, when it sails about with the utmost facility. It is a heavy, stupid bird, and sleeps much upon the water.

Pelecanus Carbo (the common corvorant) appeared only on one occasion, in a flock of six. It is thought to be rare hereabouts.

Larus Maximus, (burgomaster, or the white-winged gull.) Bill, pale yellow, with a blackish band across near the tip; body, wings and tail, snowy white, with a dash of pearly gray on the interscapular region and tertials; legs and feet, pale flesh colour; hind toe, small; claws, horn-colour; length, when full grown, thirty-two inches. Being now *for the first time described*, I have adopted the English specific name proposed by Mr. W. Bullock, of the Egyptian Hall, Piccadilly; in whose museum the bird is placed. The name of burgomaster is that by which it is familiarly known among the Greenland men.

The white-winged gull is generally solitary; most likely the female being then, namely, in June, in the state of incubation; but, in the latter end of the summer, they sometimes appear in pairs, attended by one young one. This bird seems to partake of a quality remarkable to all large animals—an indolence, or love of ease: his mode of flight indicates this disposition. A continued, slow and heavy stroke, carries him forward with a speed much greater than one would suppose from his motion. His more bustling and voracious neighbour, the mallemuck, gives him no concern; and that quarrelsome gourmand is never seen to interfere with the purposes of his gigantic companion. The larus maximus, however, frequents the places where the offals of whales may be found; but he is extremely shy, and carefully keeps at a great distance. His cry is pleasing, weak, and plaintive, yet may be heard a good way off.

Larus Eburneus, (the ivory gull, or ice bird.) This truly beautiful bird has the plumage as white as snow when full grown; but the young are elegantly diversified with spots of black. Eye, jet black; bill and legs, lead colour; sixteen inches long. This bird, so pleasing to the observer, is sure to torture him with its perpetual and disagreeable screaming.

Larus Canus (common gray gull) is not frequently seen. The same may be observed of the L. cataractes, or skua gull, and also of the L. fuscus, or herring gull.

Larus Tridactylus (kittiwake or tarrock) is very numerous in Davis's Strait. The trivial name is derived from its cry, which is a shrill scream, somewhat resembling the word kittiwake. It may be known from the young ivory gull, by the bill being yellowish, and the mouth of a saffron colour within.

Larus Parysiticus (arctic gull, or boatswain.) This bird is very rapacious, pursuing the weaker gulls until fear from continued pursuit causes them to discharge what they have eaten, which it dexterously catches and devours before it can reach the water. The two middle tail feathers are very long, but the females are said to be destitute of this mark: many of the species being seen together, a few only have those remarkable feathers. The boatswain is very fond of flying round the penants of the ships, but no cause can be assigned for this singular habit. Its colour is generally brown.

Stuna Hirundo, (the greater tern.) This beautiful bird is seen in great numbers, sometimes thousands together, resting on an ice berg, and, when on wing, exhibits a graceful and elegant flight. The S. hirundo seeks its food, which is mostly the clio retusa, or some other mollusca, by plunging into the water sometimes six inches and more, at which depth that little clio plies his flimsy oar in company with the gaudy medusa pileus, and others of that genus. The tern, or as it is called the sea-swallow, is in flesh not much larger than a lark, though to the extremity of its forked tail it measures twelve inches. The wings are very long and light; bill and legs, crimson; the former tipped with black; cap and ocular band, black; back and wings, cinereous; outer tail-feathers, edged with black; rest of the body white.

Colymbus Troile, (foolish guillemot.) Immense flocks of these birds annually visit Davis's Strait; but they seldom go much further north than the seventy-third degree. The sailors give them the name of looms. The body is black; breast and belly, snowy; secondary quill feathers, tipped with white; bill, black and slender, the edges sharp and compressed, and covered with short feathers at the base. This last character is distinctive of the genus. The loom is eagerly chased by the Uskee-mè, who finds in such pursuit the highest gratification. When approaching to strike the loom, the Uskee stoops very low, his chin almost resting on the kaiak, paddling with his left hand, and, with his dart ready in his right, he advances singing or whistling low and pleasing notes, whilst the bird, justly called the foolish guillemot, rather amused than alarmed, awaits his pursuer's approach, who, from his singular accuracy of aim, and experience of distance, seldom fails to strike his object. The warm blood of the loom is a delicious cordial on the occasion, and the flesh a ready repast. The skin is much prized as material for inside dress, for which it is certainly well calculated, from the depth of the plumage. A proof of the estimation in which this little capture is held among the Greenlanders is their unwillingness to barter those birds with Europeans, the highest compliment being an offer of truck for one of them. The loom is seventeen inches in length.

Colymbus Grylle, (black guillemot, or dovekee.) The many changes of plumage which this bird puts on, from variety of climate, and such other circumstances as sway its habits, admit a description only of its general characters. Body above, sooty black; wing coverts, white, or white intermixed with light-brown; body beneath, white; bill, black and long; inside of the mouth and legs, red; length, from twelve to fourteen inches.

The habits of the dovekee are scarcely different from those of the loom. Like the latter, it is gregarious: but seldom joining in society with others of the genus. No evident hostility forbids association among those devotees of gluttony; yet they are found invariably separated in flocks of distinct species. An odd dovekee is sometimes observed among the throng of Col. glocitans, and that in their most northern migration. Sea being the dovekee's home, this bird has little intercourse with land, except for the purpose of incubation. Its nest is on the ground exposed, and merely temporary; always near the grand retreat. This dwelling is extremely simple, and formed of such adjacent materials as the site will supply. Tenant at will, the dovekee seeks not for much luxury; and the whole of its active life seems to be similar to that of the human lord who derives his scanty and precarious sustenance from the same waters, in the same situation.

Colymbus Glocitans, (the roch.) *This bird is new in description*, and is peculiarly remarkable from its frequency and softness of call. Hence it merits the specific name which I have ventured to assign it. Bill, short and black; both mandibles, arched, the edges compressed and sharp; head, neck and body above, sooty black; wings, light-brown, irregularly mixed with white; bill and scapulars, white; legs, black; length, when fully grown, ten inches.

The roch is the remotest and last visiter of Davis's Strait, which it frequents in immense flocks, darkening the surface of the sea, and with its incessant call enlivening that dreary scene, where nature seems wrapped in eternal slumber. In view of the Linnæan Isles, the water is covered with millions of this species, where their favourite food, the clio retusa, abounds. Sometimes an individual dovekee is seen in the throng, or the majestic and solitary burgomaster. When the returning sun warns for general departure, the roch is the last to disappear. Ordinarily its flight is low, close to the surface of the sea, which in that high latitude, during the summer months, is mostly calm; but when migrating, the flock assumes an elevation of about a quarter of a mile, and may, at any distance in sight, be distinguished by its rapid and hurried movement.

This bird employs both wings and webbed feet when under the surface of the water. Often, when suddenly overtaken, have I seen them make such exertion, plunging in a twinkling, and, rowing away from the cause of alarm, yet not forgetful of their purpose, seize the flimsy clio in their progress. On emerging, they are able at once to take flight, which facility they derive from the abundance of oil which they possess. The flesh is esteemed good. This predilection may proceed from a desire to enjoy fresh meat; and an apprehension may be entertained that few delicate appetites would relish a pye formed of a bird of its unsavoury habits.

Many other subjects in the zoology of Greenland remain to be described; but I beg leave to refer the reader, for the more minute ones, to the accurate work of Fabricius, Fauna Grænlandica, where will be found interesting and elegant descriptions of animals collected in the course of many years' observation.

One circumstance, however, I must not omit, as it offers an explanation in natural history hitherto desired. A species of squalus is to be met with in Davis's Strait, by sailors called the blind shark, which is supposed to be an applicable name, from the temerity with which the animal, regardless of his own safety, rushes to his prey. This shark is about four feet in length, body dark blue, shaded with brown on the sides, and is very steady and slow in movement. A whale (B. M.) having been killed, and made fast alongside the ship, the men being in the act of flinching, one of these sharks came up, and fastened on the body, with a circular scoop cutting out the part seized, and whilst so engaged, bore to be stabbed several times by one of the ship-boys. The assertion, therefore, that the shark turns on the back for the purpose of snapping his prey is incorrect. That effect is produced by the sweep in the circular revolution, by which the numerous rows of the angular and edged teeth in the jaws of the animal are brought into successive action. It is probable that it was in observing the body of the shark up-turned in this revolution that the error first arose.

CHAPTER VI.

ON THE EFFECTING OF A NORTH-WEST PASSAGE.

SINCE these pages were commenced, I have been informed by the newspapers, that ships are fitting out by orders of the Admiralty to explore a passage to the Pacific Ocean through the arctic seas. The reader will excuse the insertion here of an article that appeared to that effect. I do not wish to load my page with quotations; but this seems of some importance, as it refers to the first authority on this subject.

"We learn that a vessel is to be fitted out by Government for the purpose of attempting again the north-west passage, the season being considered as peculiarly favourable to such an expedition. Our readers need not be informed that larger masses of ice than ever were before known have this year been seen floating in the Atlantic, and that from their magnitude and solidity, they reached even the fortieth latitude before they were melted into a fluid state. From an examination of the Greenland captains, it has been found that, owing to some convulsions of nature, the sea was more open and more free from compact ice than in any former voyage they ever made; that several ships actually reached the eighty-fourth degree of latitude, in which no ice whatever was found; that, for the first time for 400 years, vessels penetrated to the west coast of Greenland, and that they apprehended no obstacle to their even reaching the pole, if it had consisted with their duty to their employers to make the attempt. This curious and important information has, we learn, induced the Royal Society to apply to ministers to renew the attempt of exploring a north-west passage, as well as to give encouragement to fishing vessels to try how far northward they can reach, by dividing the bounty to be given, on the actual discovery, into portions, as a reward for every degree beyond eighty-four that they shall penetrate. For the same reason, we think it would be adviseable for the merchants engaged in the Greenland whale fishery not to postpone the sailing of their ships to the usual season, but expedite them at once so as to take advantage of the temporary fresh."

In addition to the above, another notification informs the public, that

"Capt. Buchan, of the Pike sloop of war, recently returned from Newfoundland, is appointed to the expedition to the north pole. Capt. Ross is the other officer who proceeds thither. They are to be accompanied by four lieutenants, one attached to each of the captains, and the others to command the two vessels to act as tenders. Two of the ships, as we before stated, proceed up Davis's Strait, the extent or termination of which is utterly unknown, and the other two direct, if possible, to the pole, between Iceland and Greenland. The ships are to be ready for sea by the first week in March."

Now, if these notifications convey the information on which the intended expeditions are directed, as some doubt possesses my mind on the accuracy of that information, I shall submit to public consideration a few remarks on this head, and shall afterwards briefly set before the reader an accurate journal of some months' traversing of Davis's Strait noted faithfully by myself.

Every information coming by newspaper account carries, from the abuse of some such publications, strong features of want of authenticity; but, in the present instance, where the names of captains in the navy, of most reputable character, are introduced, no doubt can exist as to the fact of the expeditions being in preparation. These notifications, however, would imply that the direction is fixed towards the north pole: such a project cannot be grounded on what has been found from an examination of the Greenland captains, who are reported to assert that, "owing to some convulsions of nature, the sea was more open and more free from compact ice than in any former voyage they ever made." The masters of whale ships are forbidden by a solemn oath,* which

* I . . . . master of the ship . . . . make oath, that it is really and truly my firm purpose, and determined resolution, that the said ship shall, as soon as license shall be granted, forthwith proceed so manned, furnished, and accoutred, on a voyage to the Greenland seas, or Davis's Strait, or the seas adjacent, there in the now approaching season, to use the utmost endeavour of myself and ship's company, to take whales or other creatures living in the seas, and on no other design or view of profit, in my present voyage, and to import the whale fins, oil, and blubber thereof into the port of . . . . Sworn, &c. at the Custom House . . . . . &c.

they must subscribe to, in the Custom House, before clearing out the voyage, to seek nothing but blubber; and this oath, or its reward from their owners, if faithfully kept in view, unfits them for affording proper or satisfactory information to philosophical inquiry. The trite vulgar phrase, "for want of a better that must do," applies to such an investigation with no complimentary effect. If accurate information be desirable on this important subject, why derive it from such erroneous chance, wherein the binding of a parliamentary oath forbids the deponent to know any thing of the matter?

The reader will look with surprise at such language as the following, conveying information on an important and philosophic subject, "Masses of ice, larger than ever before known, were seen floating in the Atlantic, and from their magnitude and solidity, reached the fortieth degree of latitude before they were melted into a fluid state." It cannot be imagined that such a story would recommend a sensible application to any persons knowing the nature of ice. The specific gravity of that substance is lighter than that of water: ice floats in fresh water, which is much lighter than salt or seawater; and chemical observation has proved that one of the chief causes of its buoyancy in the latter fluid is from the mass losing its salt, which precipitates as the congelation proceeds. Another objection to the sufficiency of this account is derivable from the terms "solid," and "compact," when applied to ice; for surely no philosophic mind would find it right to admit such phraseology in any grave representation. Again, "the

Greenland whale fishery," inserted in such a communication, would be matter of curious reading to persons knowing that whales are not scientifically denominated fish. Equally unfit would it be to represent, in such an application, that "it would be adviseable for the merchants engaged in the Greenland whale fishery, not to postpone the sailing of their ships to the usual season, but to expedite them at once, so as to take advantage of the temporary fresh." The adviser of such expediting should be aware that the ice in the arctic seas breaks up only about a certain period, in the latter end of the month of April or beginning of May, of which event the whalers are so well aware, that the Davis's Strait ships are sent off only in the beginning of March, that the length of time necessary for traversing the Atlantic may suit the usual opening of the ice; whereas those "expedited" for the Spitzbergen sea are detained nearly a month later. Besides, those who would be directed by such an advice ought to be aware that no such thing as a temporary fresh exists in the northern seas. The current is steadily and uniformly southward; and the great expanse of those waters gives such room for the diffusion of ice reduced to its liquid origin, and the accession of the streams issuing from the numerous fiords and rivers, that such a fresh is never experienced. The sage solution of St. Pierre, with regard to the supply of material for the daily rise of the tide, is less reprehensible, but equally speculative. The delightful novelist just mentioned, sitting in his closet, remarked the influence of the sun as differing very materially during the day and night.

The force of imagination made him conclude that from the unknown seas around the north pole, a diurnal supply could be derived from the action of the sun upon the ice. In convincing himself that the sun's rays actually dissolve ice, and that the light and influence of that globe is communicated to our earth once every twenty-four hours, the succession of the ebb and flow twice in that period became evident. The tides as experienced, however, in more southern latitudes should be, from such cause, only two every year, or, at least, there should be a very remarkable increase only when the solution of polar ice is complete, which should be in the middle of August, while it should be very low when the surface of the polar seas is bound in its wintry coat, which is most solid and unbroken in February.

To be acquainted with the arctic seas, one must visit those regions; for, from my own experience, I assert, that in no other way can a useful and accurate knowledge of the subject be obtained. It is quite absurd that persons not accustomed to sea should undertake a demarkation of a ship's course, directing a certain line of longitude to be adhered to, as was dictated to the late Lord Mulgrave. Such sapience is as much to be admired as that of the Roman Pontiff who cut out the Brazils from South America in a similar manner. Those who know the arctic seas are aware of the impossibility of adhering to such an order; and it is to be hoped that, for the safety of the crews, and the success of the intended expeditions, such a tying up of hands will not be insisted on. When the subject hereafter may admit of a full delineation of its difficulties and dangers, to which I presume the facts of the following Journal* may be deemed properly antecedent, the above intimation will be found not irrelevant to the expedition.

Considering here only the more generally interest-

* JOURNAL IN DAVIS'S STRAIT.

Thursday, May 8: thermometer 20°, 18°, 12°: wind S. W., strong breeze: off Disko Bay: two whales seen, and one seal: cirrostratus in haze, and some more dense lower down: some natives, each carrying his canoe on his head, passed over the ice, and visited two ships which were in-shore flinching: some very large bergs in sight surrounded by field ice: the cold this evening increased very much; snow fell at times, thick and hard.

May 9: ther. 15°, 25°, 16°: wind S. E., fresh breeze: much snow fell during the preceding night: appearance of cloud cirrus fine, comoid and undulate: cirrocumulus and cirrostratus during the day, apparently near Disko, yet many miles distant from that Island: thermometer exceedingly variable throughout the course of the day, till 10 p. m. when the last observation was noted: in the evening a yellowish white cloak of cirrostratus was spread over the summit of Disko: this colour is invariably communicated to the atmosphere where bergy ice is present: larus maximus and procellaria glacialis in scanty number, also a very few of larus tridactylus: thermometer at midnight 12°.

May 10: ther. 19°, 16°, 15°: wind S., light breeze: freezing intensely: sea nearly tranquil; the surface congealed in extensive fields, which are interrupted by spaces kept free by the action of the wind: cumulostratus to the eastward; a fine, highly illumined stratus to the southward; all else clear of cloud, but of a milky blue: the light intolerable to the eye: at 8 a. m. the

ing circumstances of my journal, I may observe that, at Lievely, which we approached on the 12th of May, the Danish government keeps a colony under the superintendance of an officer, whose chief residence is said to be at the whale islands, and under his direction other agents or factors take care of the in-

influence of the sun having raised a light vapour from the surface of the ice, this became immediately condensed by the intense cold; and, drifting along the surface of the water in irregular spires, whenever met with, was found to be a cloud of minute icy particles, extremely annoying; and, from its effects, styled by the sailors, "the barber:" snow at times: day ended with icy snow.

May 11: 15°, 25°, 16°: wind S. S. E., fresh to strong breeze: cold less than on the preceding day: atmosphere at times loaded with milky haze; which, on clearing, afforded a view of beautiful snowy cirrocumulus, and in its aggregation exhibiting a changing variety of cirrostratus: close in with Disko, westward of Fortune Bay, some huge bergs embedded in flaws of field ice many miles in extent: larus marinus, procellaria glacialis, colymbus troile.

May 12: ther. 20°, 24°, 20°: wind from W. to S. E., fresh breeze: trailing masses of cumulus passed frequently across the sky: cumulostratus, and occasionally cirrocumulus seen: extensive flaws descending from the northward with a strong current, the ice being about two feet in thickness: Lievely Point not far distant: the whale islands lying to the S. W.: procellaria glacialis, corvus corax, and some ducks observed.

May 13: ther. 25°, 33°, 24°: wind variable from N. E. to N. W., fresh breeze: cirrostratus in mist: a long spreading sheet in N. E. and very dark linear parallel layers of the same in E.: the horizon exhibits a characteristic instance of ice blink. The procellaria glacialis this day active, and in vast number: some rain preceded a short fall of snow in the evening.

terests of the government, which are chiefly maintained by the industry of the natives, and Danish convicts sent thither for their offences at home. This policy is not obviously calculated to improve the condition of the poor Greenlanders, nor to aid materially the labours of the missionaries. The efforts of those

May 14: ther. 24°, 38°, 26°: wind, nearly calm, variable to S.: in the southward a heap of cumulostratus: the summits intensely white: brown and white cirrostratus floating slowly over the summit of Disko: weather at noon mild and pleasant: in the afternoon the state of atmosphere was a light grayish brown haze, blending land, ice and sea, into one immeasurable field; and, with the exception of the summit of Disko, making the scene interminable.

May 15: ther. 30°, 31°, 32°: wind calm throughout: sun in a dim corona: misty brown cirrostratus creeping along the breast of Disko, about half of its elevation: sea still and smooth: several very large seals seen, but too cautious to be come at.

May 16: ther. 31°, 34°, 27°: wind W., light breeze: some snow and rain, at intervals sleet: weather mild: ship in company with many others at Fortune Point, made fast to a berg: saw a fox and a bear this day: in the valley west of Fortune Bay, a flood of cirrostratus, in snowy fleeces, spilling down from the summit of the mountain: cirrus.

May 17: ther. 34°, 51°, 36°: wind calm: in Love Bay, at Disko, lat. observed 69° 10′ N.: the atmosphere heated very much towards the afternoon: the cirrus radiation, as heretofore observed, occurred this evening, at a great elevation, running from the southward.

May 18: ther. 40°, 50°, 34°: wind, light air and variable from N.: at 8 p. m. wind increased in the same point to fresh breeze, which was pre-indicated by the radiation of last day: extensive but loose cirrocumulus slightly obscuring the sun: ship

benevolent pastors are much counteracted by the abandoned habits of the convicts, who intermarry with the natives; and, as the latter now are convinced, endeavour to debase the national character. "Those strangers," they say, "are helpless and bad; know not the use of the paddle or dart, and if left to them-

still fast to ice in Love Bay: coarse sand in seventeen fathoms of sounding.

The tide rises here about eight feet: the ice began now slowly moving down to the southward, and shut in the point of Lievely: a shoal of delphinus leucas seen, each about ten feet in length: a pair of ravens seen.

May 19: ther. 32°, 34°, 28°: wind N., light breeze: general diffusion of brownish-gray cirrostratus: the sun light intense, allows a distinct view of objects the most distant: Disko clear: atmosphere mildly warm: ship cast off from the ice as it began to open freely: course directed to the N. W. as all the South-East Bay and the Waygat Sound were closed, according to the report of the natives: one blubber whale and a seal seen: also a raven, a few looms, and a small number of procellaria glacialis on wing, proceeding to the north-westward.

May 20: ther. 26°, 32°, 34°: wind, a light air from S.: atmosphere loaded with vapoury cirrostratus, variously coloured by the sun-light; the ice blink very remarkable where an ice berg lies in the horizon: about noon the cloud cleared up under the strong influence of the sun, forming cirrus alternating with cirrocumulus: a light brown cirrus radiation appeared in the westward, rising from an interrupted chain of cirrostratous patches, which formed the segment of a circle, having its centre towards the zenith: this curve became reversed as the radiation dispersed, the centre then being towards the horizon: the wind blew a fresh breeze from that point after an interval of nearly four hours: in this part of the Strait the wind is very variable, and seldom of long duration: at midnight the sun just reached the

selves must starve." European vices, through such means, have also found their way to the huts of this harmless people; and even the bargains effected by their governors are so severe upon their miserable means, as to make them little satisfied of their sense of justice.

horizon, shrouded in a deep brown mantle of cirrostratus, with a rich reddish-brown border next the water; above and around were beautiful exhibitions of cirrocumulus and cirrus, some retaining their forms for a long time, and others imperceptibly interchanging shapes: the moon appeared distinctly at a great elevation in the N. W.* It is remarked among the whalers, that when the moon appears in those latitudes, it is a sure indication of foul weather: in the present case, however, this assurance was found to be incorrect.

May 21: ther. 39°, 42°, 32°: wind perfectly calm: morning delightfully fine, such as would appear most charming to the senses, if the beauties of vegetation were added to the scene: sun-light intensely bright: not a speck of cloud to be seen: Disko in the distance unclouded: packs of ice all around: the whale boats busy in every direction, a few of what are called "straggling fish" having appeared: the whales so seen were running rapidly in many directions, but chiefly towards the north-west. Many seals continued sporting in view this evening: a few looms, but no other birds seen.

May 22: ther. 32°, 42°, 30°: wind S. S. W., light breeze from variable: Disko crowned with brown cirrostratus: others appear in profile pointing north and south: the day continued unusually fine: procellaria glacialis, larus tridactylus and canus in small number: a few seals appeared, but were evidently very cautious, from the habitual persecution of the natives.

May 23: ther. 28°, 33°, 32°: wind N. E. shifting to S. W., fresh breeze: dark vapoury cirrostratus, and others in profile,

* All bearings mentioned in this journal are by compass.

On a prominent eminence at Lievely stands a wooden building, called a look-out house, the standing place of such persons as are on the watch for whales. The house of the governor, which is also built of wood, is in a sheltered situation. There is also a large building reserved as a store-house for the fishing im-

pointing northward : larus maximus seen : at ten p. m. a beautiful parhelion appeared above Disko. This phenomenon, which is commonly named a mock sun, exhibited two distinct portions of an iridescent circle surrounding that luminary, and parallel to the line of the horizon : no portion of such light as the sun affords, but the brilliant colours of the rainbow, were reflected from the sun's light upon a deep brown bed of cirrostratus, through which the sun light broke, affecting those colours in its passage through the cloud : it is quite erroneous to apply the name of mock sun to such a phenomenon ; it might be equally assigned to the rainbow. A seal was shot, but the body sunk before a boat could be lowered down to seize it.

May 24 : ther. 26°, 42°, 36° : wind S. W., fresh breeze : ship moving among packed ice off Fortune Bay : light snow sometimes falling : a dense ledge of cirrostratus in N. W. : larus marinus, tridactylus and eburneus, in considerable numbers around ; L. maximus, as usual, a solitary individual : procellaria glacialis in great number : ursus maritimus ; one killed to-day.

May 25 : ther. 37°, 42°, 35° : wind N. E., light breeze : atmosphere clear and dry : Disko unclouded : cirrus and cirrocumulus at a very great elevation : a fog bank, which is a dense and extensive accumulation of cirrostratus, appeared to the northward : this is said to be stationary for several days, and when moving, proceeds like the thunder-cloud against the wind : weather fine : this day a swell of the sea was observed by the whalers, and hailed with joy, because it helps to heave the surface so irregularly as to cause the field ice to break up : it is produced by a gale blowing in some remote quarter some days before : the direction of the swell could not as yet be ascertained, as it was

plements, and for the other purposes of the colony. The materials for these buildings are conveyed from Europe, but not always in sufficient supply for the wants of the people, who have frequently a very providential relief in the drifted pines and other timbers that are occasionally driven on their shores; but

scarcely perceptible: the fog bank dispersed within a few hours: sterna hirundo: Lievely bearing S. E. by S., distant six or seven leagues, soundings were taken, twelve, twenty, and forty fathoms, though the common sailing chart states the depth in this place to be 130 fathoms: there is a dangerous difference between.

May 26: ther. 29°, 32°, 30°: wind W. S. W., strong breeze: the still and tranquil state of the last fortnight is much changed since the appearance of the swell noticed last evening: the ice has undergone much dissolution, and extensive seas are now visible amongst the packs: the swell came from the southward, and was more determined towards midnight, when the atmosphere became loaded with snow-cloud, which was succeeded by cirrostratus flying along with much velocity: in the higher regions cirrus and cirrocumulus uninfluenced by the wind, agitating the mass below. The rock of Disko, in the distance, appeared as if standing on a mirror, though the ice was visible close in with the shore, and extended outwards in a close pack for leagues: the snow channels down the rock seemed to be perpendicular to the plane of the imaginary mirror: larus maximus, canus, and marinus on wing: P. glacialis; also a raven.

May 27: ther. 32°, 34°, 36°: wind, light airs, variable: comoid cirrus, and streaks of cirrostratus in the horizon pointing to N. W. and S. E.: ship cleared the ice and moved into the vicinity of the Whale, Dog and Western Isles: colymbus troile.

May 28: ther. 42° throughout: wind S. E., fresh breeze: cirrus varying its forms incessantly, its fine points directed to S. W.: afternoon still and calm: surface of the sea of glassy smoothness, dimpled only by the plunge of the sterna hirundo, which plied its graceful wing all around: colymbus troile sometimes

whence this wood comes, a thorough investigation of the Greenland currents only can determine.

The ice blink, seen by us on the 13th, is a dull yellowish light just above the horizon; and, more elevated, a haze of a gray but piercing light, exceedingly distressing to the sight. Objects, such as ships, leave

seen, also a numerous train of anas mollissima ; three very large sized balæna physalus, passed with their usual speed, followed by a busy herd of delphinus leucas : the blast of the finner could be distinctly heard five or six seconds after its visible elevation : this evening nine natives put off from the Western Islands, and came alongside the ship to traffick : after some hours' stay, during which time a young man showed his skill in striking a loom, they departed : they were very different from each other in features, but were all evidently of the aboriginal race : a seal happening to appear near one, he instantly pursued the animal, and the others sat watching his success, and, upon his striking his object, which he did with great address, the rest paddled hastily to his assistance, but the seal escaped.

May 29 : ther. 36°, 46°, 31° : wind E., fresh breeze : atmosphere clear and cloudless : Disko dipping in the horizon : some whales have been seen in S. W. of Fish Bay : seawater deep brown, with a greenish tinge : wherever the water appears of this colour, it is considered the whale's feeding-place : a brilliant parhelion seen at a little before midnight.

May 30 : ther. 30°, 48°, 32° : wind E., light breeze : a swell from S. W. : cirrus and cirrocumulus, the former in beautiful variety : the ice blink remarkably oppressive this day, being a dull, milky, but powerful light : a blubber whale killed this day measured upwards of fifty feet : thousands of mallemucks crowded round the ship to partake of the spoil : the whale-bone measured ten feet and one inch.

May 31 : ther. 30°, 33°, 30° : wind N. E., strong breeze : this day gave me a full opportunity of observing a whale moving at will : ascending from the bottom, this enormous animal arose just

an impression on the eye, in the medium of this ice blink, so that whichever way the spectator turns, he beholds the same objects still represented to his vision. Bergs similar to islands, having bold and precipitous fronts, sometimes crowned with eminences like rocks or castles, and the summit of this seeming land sloping

under the stern of the ship, and moved forwards in a majestic style, having taken in fresh air, and descended forwards slowly again : its motions were effected with much ease, though the speed is so great, being between eight and nine, sometimes ten miles an hour : the whales are generally seen at this date in pairs, or three together, two probably rival suitors for the female's regard.

Weather beginning to grow thick : the circle of view, however, is large : the ice much dispersed, and in active dissolution : colymbus glocitans in considerable number : colymbus troile, few : larus canus and tridactylus : procellaria glacialis less numerous than usual.

June 1 : ther. 32°, 48°, 30° : wind N. E., light breeze : the misty cirrostratus continued since last, congealing into rime as it drifted across the ship : a male whale fifty-eight feet long was killed this day : procellaria glacialis again in immense number : larus maximus, eburneus, tridactylus and marinus.

June 2 : ther. 32°, 34°, 33° : wind E., strong breeze : cirrostratus in mist : a male whale killed this morning measured seventy feet, the longest lamina eleven feet three inches : whilst the men were engaged flinching this huge body, a blind shark came, and in its over anxious desire to share of the spoil, gave one of the boys an opportunity of wounding him several times : groups of the oniscus ceti, whale louse, attached to the epidermis of this whale, particularly about the fins and anus.

June 3 : ther. 32°, 37°, 30° : wind nearly calm.

June 4 : ther. 32° throughout : wind N. E., light air.

June 5 : ther. 27°, 38°, 32° : wind E., light breeze.

June 6 : ther. 38°, 56°, 38° : wind E. N. E., light air.

June 7 : ther. 30°, 36°, 33° : wind nearly calm.

gradually the opposite way, lie around embedded in the field ice; but being so much deeper, they are more influenced by the current, which, pressing forward against this huge mass, forces it to rive the surrounding field, and produce the flaw ice, which is then carried off by the current, and pushed on by the ma-

June 8 : ther. 31°, 36°, 34° : wind N. E., strong breeze.

The weather during the above days had scarcely any variety, and could afford little information or amusement to the reader; the atmosphere being generally loaded with heavy vapour, and sometimes acicular snow : sea almost clear of ice : ship to the westward of Disko about thirty miles distant.

June 9 : ther. 42°, 53°, 43° : wind S. E., fresh breeze : atmosphere clear and dry; Whale Islands to the S. E. in sight: light feathery cirrus, with faintly marked cirrocumulus, and a dash of cirrostratus brown mist, flittering far beneath : a hugely headed whale sixty feet long was harpooned amongst some bay ice, that is, ice recently formed in some bay and carried out to sea: such ice is the thinnest description of congelation which is covered with snow, and readily dissolves: the snow nearly dissolved from the face of Disko, which is now mostly of a dark brown appearance : at noon the air was exceedingly sultry, wind same time S. W. : a few threads of cirrus seen in the afternoon, with others of comoid character arising out of them, and passing to some distance at right angles : mallemucks numerous ; burgomasters, a pair ; terns and kittiwakes around.

Between eight and twelve o'clock p. m. having in this interval kept constantly looking at the patches of ice, among which the boats were busied in pursuit of numerous whales, the colour of the ice, as it appeared to my sight, surprised me very much, assuming at a distance a bright pink, and in situations nearer to the eye a pale purple. There was no cloud over head, nor any visible, except a yellowish brown stratus occupying the whole horizon. This phenomenon I do not recollect to see noticed by any person heretofore.

jestic berg. The flaw ice, sometimes leagues in extent, invariably level, and covered with snow about ten inches deep, is also urged in its change of place by the pressure of the wind, which, though probably not blowing at one extremity of the flaw, produces its preponderating effects at the other. Masters of ships

June 10: ther. 31°, 46°, 28°: wind N. E., light breeze: to the fine weather of the last, a dark, chill atmosphere has succeeded, loaded with icy vapour; but this state of atmosphere is evidently confined to a low degree, as the zenith remains clear: at noon more clear around, and cirrus, with cirrocumulus of brilliant white, occupied the higher region: the mist afterwards returned, general and dense, and is likely to continue, the wind growing to a strong breeze, with a heavy sea.

This mist, or fog, was produced by the great heat of the preceding day, when the ice continued to dissolve freely; and the vapour thence arising, became material for the fog which was condensed by the wind at N. E.: this circumstance deserves attention, and shows the importance to the mariner of his possessing himself of such indications as may enable him to anticipate such changes. The loss of many a ship every year may be ascribed principally to want of attention, and proper information on this head.

Procellaria glacialis numerous: colymbus troile in long trains: sterna hirundo and larus eburneus also numerous.

June 11: ther. 27°, 34°, 30°: wind N. E., strong breeze: this day continues very cold, the fog still remaining, at intervals clearing partially, and returning thick again, depositing rounded tapering crystals, of a large size, upon the ropes: these crystals are formed by the successive deposition of minute icy particles from the fog: before noon the cloud assumed a greater elevation, so as to leave the horizon clear: the atmosphere cold and dark: P. glacialis and L. eburneus.

June 12: ther. 32°, 47°, 33°: wind E. N. E., fresh breeze: fog still continuing, strongly illuminated by the sun-light; about 4 p. m. there was some appearance of clearing up, but the fog again

are cautious of remaining in such a situation as places them in the course in which the flaw is observed to move; but this caution springs from experience alone, as the water about the flaw, particularly if the ship lie on the sheltered side, erroneously named the windward, is usually very tranquil. Then, unless the ut-

resumed its former dense character: procellaria glacialis, colymbus modulans, and sterna hirundo.

June 13: ther. 30°, 52°, 40°: wind, light and variable: the fog having cleared away to the S. E. all the sky is clear: ship a short distance from Fortune Bay: no ice to be seen, except a few bergs. Just over Disko appeared a milk-white haze forming rapidly into small light patches of cirrostratus in a circular line, out of which white radiations stretched through the atmosphere, with visible motion, the centre of radiation lying in the E. point, per compass. This radiation continued during the day, extending over the whole upper sky, in fine lengthened cirrus hairs of the brightest whiteness. These latter towards evening gradually assumed a greater elevation, exhibiting a beautiful display of the varieties of that delicate cloud, the trains pointing to the S. W. from which quarter others more faint issued, as if to meet the former. Latterly a dead calm prevailed, and some appearance of the recurrence of the fog: procellaria glacialis sitting on the water all around, and immense numbers of sterna hirundo on the wing: the cry of the latter is a shrill scream.

June 14: ther. 34°, 46°, 32°: wind S. E., light air: fog, with light minute snow drops: afternoon, a dead calm: a group of seals passed, flaunting along, seemingly in high fun: the sailors give such assemblages the whimsical appellation of "seals' weddings:" procellaria glacialis, larus tridactylus and canus: also colymbus troile in vast number: a pair of colymbus grylle: the numerous flock of sterna hirundo reappeared with their usual clamour: their cry is uttered when about to make the plunge,

most care be taken, the shifting flaw will force the ship from her station, sometimes to a dangerous extent; when, if rocks intervene, and arrest her in the drifting, destruction is inevitable, as the superior weight of ice will certainly upset or sink her.

Many dangerous reefs and sunken rocks, which

which is often to a considerable depth below the surface of the water, and they seldom miss their object.

June 15: ther. 30°, 40°, 38°: wind light air from S., and calm: cirrostratus irregularly scattered at an elevation of about half a mile: about 7 p. m. a breeze sprung up from N. E. increasing as the day advanced: a merry emigration of seals, more than twenty in number, was observed, and seemed to enjoy the notice taken of their glee: larus maximus, four seen this day, and a countless number of other aquatic birds; among these a single pair of the eider duck.

June 16: ther. 30°, 34°, 30°: wind N. E., strong breeze; no land in sight: ice blink in N. W.: cirrostratus irregularly diffused: atmosphere gloomy, but not sensibly cold, even at noon: a herd of whales was seen, moving together in a breast line: a group of seals formed a similar line in their advance, whilst numerous sportive stragglers filled up their rear: procellaria glacialis numerous, active, and unusually bold, which latter character this bird always assumes around the ships, when whales are in the vicinity: also larus maximus; the breeze and dark weather continued to the end.

June 17: ther. 30°, 46°, 40°: wind E. S. E., fresh breeze: in the forenoon, the atmosphere continued dark, cold and hazy, with light acicular snow: the ice blink of the preceding day covered an immense pack, which is supposed, at this date, to extend to the western continent: numerous bergs, of enormous size, sate in various directions amongst this ice: the removal of this ice from the shores of Greenland, is, in consequence of the prevalence of the easterly winds, aided by so much of the north wind and the current.

have not been laid down on the charts already published, are to be met with in those seas; but they have not been ascertained except within very few years back, at times when the boldness of the whale hunters, arising from the confidence of experience in

Afternoon the atmosphere suddenly cleared up, and became dry and fine; a few trains of brown patches of cirrostratus alone remaining, and pointing in their bases to the N. E.: the north-west side of Disko in sight, high bluff Table Land: colymbus modulans in numerous flocks, and a few of procellaria glacialis.

June 18: ther. 32°, 35°, 32°: wind N. E., strong breeze: this wind, though unfavourable to proceeding northward, is useful in driving the ice to the southward and westward, and tends to open a communication with the waters further north.

Here is an evident proof of the importance which attaches to the observation of the clouds. In the remarks of the preceding day, it may be seen that the patches of cirrostratus, in their bases, pointed to the quarter whence the succeeding wind came. This cloud may be deemed to announce the earliest wind, whilst the cirrus points to one remotely distant, and which in its coming is liable to interruption. This distinction may be of use if judiciously applied.

This period of the season is remarkable for the progress of the whale northward: heavy packs of ice, and bergs around: north-west of Disko still in sight, five or six leagues distant: upper region of atmosphere overcast with drifting cirrostratus, which clearing at intervals exhibited cirrocumulus, and subsequently cirrus: this latter cloud, at a later hour, moved off in the direction of the wind above noted; hence it is likely to continue, as it occupies so large a portion of the atmosphere: this evening afforded a clear view of the lofty peaks on the Waygat side of Disko, which towered above the mountain, as it bends its rocky prominences to the north-west: probably the highest moun-

this dangerous navigation, has carried them every succeeding season into new courses.

The fleet of whalers, above twenty in number, all tacking through the openings of the ice, making for the protection of the point of Lievely, distant about four or five miles to the S. E., and their various posi-

tain in Greenland is one of these: it rises greatly above the rest, and is visible across the whole north-west end of Disko: by calculation it must be one half as high again as the land at Fortune Bay.

June 19: ther. 32°, 36°, 34°: wind N. E., strong breeze: it is remarked, that the prevailing winds along the coast are N. or S.: for this reason the study of the minutest indication of any change of wind in these seas is imperative, as the progress of the most experienced navigator must be otherwise baffled perpetually, and the purposes of his voyage embarrassed with difficulty, doubt and danger.

At an early hour this morning the zenith was enriched by an elegant display of cirrus, in comoid, streaked, waved and minutely dotted form, all which underwent a complete and hasty dissolution, by a wind from the N. leaving a thin whey-coloured mist at a very great elevation: procellaria glacialis, colymbus troile and glocitans: the water deep brown, with greenish hue, reflecting purple when turned up in wave; this latter colour may proceed from the fragments of the frail medusa pileus, which is hereabouts in vast number.

June 20: ther. 32°, 37°, 32°: wind N. E., fresh breeze: cirrostratus at a great elevation overclouding the welkin: at noon calm and clear: comoid cirrus, and cirrocumulus, the former indicating a wind from S. W.: the calm was succeeded soon by a dense dry fog from the westward with light variable winds from that quarter: a steady fresh breeze from S. W. sprung up afterwards, when the fog cleared away, and the ship was ascertained to be in the latitude of the Mallegat, which is a short rocky sound between Disko and Hare Island: colymbus troile and larus maximus: the latter solitary.

tions, the serenity of the weather, and the magnificent brow of Disko looking down on an apparently Lilliputian scene, was certainly a novel exhibition to a stranger: even the hardy sailors viewed it with delight. Though the thermometer indicated so low a temperature, yet the air felt agreeably warm, proba-

June 21: ther. 32°, 46°, 36°: wind S. W., light breeze: morning fine with cirrostratus: Black Hook in sight: the wind being favourable, much of this part of Greenland came within view: at noon a large island was ascertained to be, by observation, in latitude 71° 46′ north; but as few parts in these latitudes, except remarkable headlands, are named, this island has not yet received any distinct name from Europeans. The rock is the same as that noticed at Disko, namely floetz trap, with a distinct stratum of feltspar, about high water mark: numerous flocks of roches, looms, dovekies, mallemucks and kittiwakes; also a solitary burgomaster.

June 22: ther. 32°, 41°, 30°: wind calm or variable and light: the transient visitation of the wind, coming at uncertain intervals, and from almost every point of the compass, produces a slight ruffling of the sea, which is throughout this day of a glassy smoothness: the sailors call these ruffled patches, cat-skins: these patches are only of short duration, and the most extensive not half a mile over: they are invariably in the corresponding position of the superincumbent cloud, which is cirrostratus, low and of a deep brown, except where the sun-light tinges it of a yellow hue: in the places where this cloud approaches the horizon, a distinct communication may be observed between the cirrostratus bed and the wave beneath, somewhat similar to rain descending from a nimbus: this communication was always followed by the cat-skin. Whenever the ship came within such communication, I observed a light mist to fall in acicular snow, exceedingly minute and evanescent.

June 23: ther. 34°, 44°, 28°: wind E. N. E., light breeze: cirrocumulus of dazzling whiteness seen through the purplish

bly from the effects of the sun on the rocks of Disko. It being expedient to make the ship fast to a berg, an anchor was buried in a large one near; but, having started from its fastening, sunk to the bottom; and being hauled up, had a large cluster of the ascidia pedunculata, with innumerable small animals attach-

brown masses of cirrostratus floating beneath: water, oceanic azure: land nearly out of sight: much loose ice to the westward: whales seen in groups of five and six, making hasty progress northward: some few seals came in view: the blue colour of the sea is supposed, in the Straits, to be reflected from a rocky bottom, and demands the utmost vigilance of the mariner: procellaria glacialis in small number on wing; so also larus maximus: colymbus glocitans, colymbus troile, larus tridactylus and eburneus; the latter very clamorous.

June 24: ther. 30°, 37°, 34°: wind N. E. by N., strong breeze: this day is bright, but hazy: light acicular snow constantly falling: the ice seen occasionally as the ship tacks in the breeze: procellaria glacialis, and colymbus grylle.

June 25: ther. 24°, 30°, 28°: wind N. E. by N., light breeze: atmosphere as yesterday, hazy, and intensely bright without snow; the change of temperature painfully felt: at times zenith clear.

June 26: ther. 32° invariably: wind S. W., strong breeze: at midnight, between this day and last, the sun came to the meridian at a variation of somewhat more than 6¼ points eastward of the compass: latitude 73° 15′ N., near Berry's Island: an appearance of cirrostratus cloud occurred, which is worthy of notice from its consequences—aggregated small clouds of irregular shapes, purplish brown, smooth, and edged with a soft yellowish illumination: distinct from each other, they appeared heavy and motionless: such clouds, I have since frequently noticed, usually appear before a gale: an immense number of whales made appearance amongst the surrounding packs of ice, and their blowing among the numerous bergs would have raised a notion that in this

ed, and involved in its base. This cluster of animals had much the appearance, at first sight, of beautiful scarlet fruit hanging by their stalks.

On the 18th an old Dane, drawn by twelve dogs, and attended by a native boy, came to truck with the ships. This visit was made the preceding midnight,

wilderness of most wintry aspect, the smoke of many a hearth was sent up from some very populous hamlet. The wind increased with heavy showers of snow and sleet, and became a strong gale as the ship came in sight of the Frow Islands: the swell of the sea, occasioned by the wind, grew to an unusual height: the ship continued steering under reefed topsails for Hickson's Bay, as well for shelter, as for the purposes of the voyage: the water a very deep brown colour; and, as it breaks upon the bergs, exhibits a reddish brown hue. The Frow Islands have been so named from the voyage of Davis, who is said to have first discovered those lands, and met with many Greenland women there in boats; frow and woman being the English and Dutch terms which respectively designate the sex. The greater number of those islands are low and flat; but many much larger are often invested with clouds; (cirrostratus;) at which time, from their extreme irregularity, scenes worthy of the strains of Ossian may be witnessed. The interior of this part is totally unknown, as the masters of whale ships, either from their owners' orders, or their own experience of danger, will never approach near to any flat land, unless previously well known; the transition from a low island to a sunken rock being sudden. The Frow Islands are a favourite summer retreat of the Uskees; and there they construct their hunting tents during June, July and August; always retiring to some sheltered situation on the higher lands, to remain for the winter.

June 27: ther. 32°, 31°, 30°: wind W. S. W., fresh breeze: sailed through a safe passage, between the outward islands, into an extensive bay, at least fifteen miles over, north of the Frow Islands: latitude observed, 73° 4′ N.: the southern extremity

if such expression be correct at this place and date, where there is no night whatever. The Dane was dressed in the Uskee costume, and was very communicative. Others of the natives came in the course of the day for the purposes of barter. Some of these were boys; and one, of Norwegian descent, had all the

of this bay I suppose to be the Hope Saunderson of former voyagers; it is distinguishable by a remarkable rock above a low island, which rock has a diamond summit: as this rock came into view in the forenoon, just as the snow storm had begun to clear, it formed the centre of a landscape singularly grand. To the right, southward, lay the Frow Islands in endless variety of shape and distance, with volumes of fog rolling slowly over their craggy summits; Saunderson's Hope rising in the middle, sometimes belted with mist, soon after capped with the same transient ornament; and to the left, sweeping eastward and northward, the bay to which I have, in compliment to the owner of the Thomas, assigned the name of Marshal's Bay.

Twenty-one ships diversified the face of this ample and secure refuge. Their figures scattered in every direction, some laid to, others moving about, in a space of fifteen miles every way, of safe, deep water: many, though near, shut from the view at times by bergs of miles in extent, whilst all was tranquil and free of danger, were, with the land view, circumstances to render the scene of deep interest.

June 28: ther. 34°, 44°, 34°: wind S. by E., light breeze: this morning clear and bright: light flakes of cirrostratus in the southern region, in strong contrast with the horizon, which was of stormy blue: this indication would portend a storm: here now every breeze is hushed, as if "nature" were endeavouring to get rid of her icy load: a lazy irregular train of cirrostratus, to the northward, creeps along the summits of the land at a very low degree, or meeting the obstruction of some greater eminence, clambers up the rock, then tumbles down the opposite side unwillingly.

The chain of islands forming Marshal's Bay is, in general cha-

erect figure and fair complexion of a European. One of these, said to be the son of the former governor, a handsome interesting lad, also brought articles of dress to exchange among the ships. He evidently had a superior manner to his companions, but exhibited an eagerness, equal to theirs, to benefit by the visit of

racter, low and rounded ; and no perpendicular, or sharp front is visible. Beyond the bosom of the bay may be seen more elevated land, with peaked summits ; but, as in the view of the land near Joris Bay, in no instance does it rise to the table level of Disko. This would lead to a far different conclusion from that drawn by a geologist of eminence. If peaked mountains be always granitic, that of Teneriffe should be so ; the southern mountains of Greenland ought to be of the same material ; so should that along the coast down to Joris Bay, and Koll Reef. But the wildly torn materials of the Greenland coast seem to defy such speculation. Greenland has its peaked mountains, not of granitic substance superiorly, but as at Disko, where the land is high and level, generally trap, floetz trap, or feltspar, with all the intermediate quartzy combinations, and such changes of colour, as the hitherto unexplained occurrence of metallic presence may occasion. Yet suppose one endeavouring to determine, from a distance, their existence, as being granitic, from a view of their conical summits, a desire to ascertain the universal application of this dogma to the northern regions should induce a more satisfactory inquiry. It is not at the Cape of Good Hope, where there is table land, nor at Teneriffe, which is much higher, nor in the Hebrides, nor Orkney Islands, nor in Iceland or the Shetland Isles, that granite is to be traced by peaked eminence. The aggregation of that rock must depend upon other principles than those of elevation ; and whichever theory maintains that aggregation best, is most entitled to respect. Invariably near the highest mark of tide in this bay, the feltspar rock, of yellowish red, is present ; and above it, the gray-brown basalt.

By an observation taken this day, the clearness of the atmos-

the ships. This youth was also drawn by dogs on a miserable looking sledge, formed rudely of broad laths, covered with a seal-skin as a seat, which was scarcely raised above the surface of the snow. None but the youth last mentioned wore any thing as covering for the head. He had a cap neatly formed of dog-skin,

phere affording an opportunity, the latitude of the ship was found to be 73° 11′ N., corresponding nearly with the northern extremity of Berry's Island, which lies westward of the bay abovementioned: the latest observation of the thermometer, this day, is standard of atmospheric heat for the nine hours subsequent to meridian time: a breeze from N. E. rather freshens, and is likely to be constant: larus maximus on wing: a pair of monodon monoceros, and afterwards a large herd of delphinus leucas, accompanied by their young, of which another group came from the ice, now descending rapidly from the northward: some whales seen: ship proceeding to the northward, in company with thirty-four others. At a distance of about eight leagues from land, after leaving the bay above-mentioned, the northern extremity of the bay showed many islands scattered in the horizon, and ending, on their southernmost extremity, in a bluff head, beneath which lay a low island: north of this, the land arose somewhat even and low, with an elevated subconical mountain in the middle of the line observed.

June 29: ther. 32°, 34°, 33°: wind N., light airs: atmosphere alternately clear and clouded with cirrostratous haze: some faint instances of linear cirrus pointing E. and W.: extremely minute acicular snow is at times observable: about eight p. m. the wind shifted towards E., but northing a little: previously the atmosphere was suffused with cirrostratus of the flimsiest kind: every breath of wind lulled to a dead calm: the ice streaming off insensibly with the current: the whole scene was characteristic of tranquillity, heightened in effect by the numerous fleet lying about in every point with all sails loose and inactive: to this suc-

but was ready to part with it for an equivalent, and would be content to return home barehead like his companions. There was a hunch-back among the number about fourteen years of age. There was no difference whatever in their dresses.

Lievely is distant from Love Bay, or Old Lievely,

ceeded a dense mist, which limited the circle of view to about a hundred yards.

June 30 : ther. 31°, 34°, 33° : wind N. E., fresh breeze : fog intensely thick, but bright : Berry's Island near, lat. 73° 10′ N. : this island takes its name from the master of a whale ship, who, having been unsuccessful in his voyage for several years, ventured alone into this latitude, where the immense number of whales gave him the means of filling his ship with ease : his good fortune continued for several years, until others of his acquaintance, having discovered the secret, followed his track, when the whales shifted from the unexpected annoyance, and retired further to the northward : Berry erected a rude obelisk, which still remains upon this island : there are many dangerous rocks at the southern and northern extremities of Berry's Island, from which it would be adviseable to keep a ship safely distant : a shoal of delphinus leucas, with their young in company, passed the ship : procellaria glacialis numerous : larus eburneus and tridactylus ; also colymbus troile, and a pair of sterna hirundo : fog continues to the end.

July 1 : ther. 24°, 33°, 30° : wind N. E., light breeze : the fog continues still very dense, leaving a deposit of minute icy particles, which, accumulating, formed aciculated crystals, resembling very exactly the thorns on the ulex (furze) : being in the vicinity of ice, during this day, the atmosphere continued in a low degree of temperature ; yet, to the sense, the cold was not severe : procellaria glacialis, colymbus troile, and a shoal of delphinus leucas : the latter is not an object considered worthy the pursuit of the whalers, as being infinitely less productive than the Bal. mysticetus ; besides they look upon such employment as quite inade-

eight miles. There is a burying-ground above the latter in a very romantic valley, where some Dutch sailors, who happened to die by drowning, have been interred. The natives use much caution in the interment of their dead, by wedging together large stones over the grave, which is commonly in the cleft of a

quate to balance the expense: for this reason they merely amuse themselves looking on at the gambols of that beautiful animal.

July 2: ther. 26°, 33°, 28°: wind N. E., fresh breeze: ship standing in for the Frow Islands: Berry's Island about ten miles to the northward: a thin stratus only visible in the horizon, with a wreck of the fog, forming a deep brown fold in the N. E.: immense bergs towering above the summits of the islands: some fine appearance of comoid cirrus at noon: the change of position of the ship was owing to the drifting of the ice, which now began to descend very rapidly, and it would be extremely dangerous to remain within its course; for which reason the ships in general sought the shelter of the islands, which might ward off the mischief: this being field ice, with a few bergs interspersed, was easily set to the westward as it came in contact with Berry's, and the outer Frow Islands: sterna hirundo, larus maximus, colymbus grylle, and procellaria glacialis: the wind southing a little of east this evening, some rain fell.

July 3: ther. 32°, 46°, 36°: wind S. S. W., steady fresh breeze: cloud, cirrostratus, gathering up from mist, and creeping along the horizon at a small elevation in dark brown, loosely compacted beds: rain at times falling, at times evanescent snow: the land to the southward of Horsehead abreast: a shoal of finners, about twenty in number, passed the ship, going with immense speed to the southward: a flock of corvorants (pelecanus carbo) flew towards land: larus maximus, and procellaria glacialis; the latter journeying singly, but numerously, to the northward: about noon a calm succeeded, which continued for some hours, when the wind sprung up at N. E., faintly increasing: latter part hazy: passed a berg which stood above the

rock, to prevent the bears and foxes from digging up the body. A notion prevails among the masters of the whale ships, that every disappointment and unfavourable accident of the voyage would ensue were they to permit any curious person to fetch the skull of a Greenlander aboard; and so strong is this absurd impres-

surface of the sea at an elevation of about 200 feet perpendicular: flaws of ice all around: lat. 73° 15′ N.

July 4: ther. 32°, 34°, 32°: wind N. E., strong breeze: the greater part of this day the weather continued chill and thick: about eight p. m. it cleared up and afforded a view of thirty sail, moving in various courses among the ice, which by the wind and tide has been broken into streams: very little northing has been obtained this day, in consequence of the contrary wind, and the descent of the ice, which it required much skilful management to keep clear of: sterna hirundo plying his delicate pinion; whilst the procellaria glacialis seemed quite at ease, cleaving the breeze without apparent effort.

July 5: ther. 32°, 38°, 35°: wind S. E., fresh breeze: the vapour, on the changing of the wind, became converted into rain, which fell incessantly for nearly twelve hours, when at ten a. m. the cloud assumed all the various forms of cirrostratus, from the light brown vapour to the densest streak: Horsehead on the ship's beam distant six miles.

Along this coast the land appears in no place flat or level, neither is the elevation of any part considerable; but the iron-coloured rock dips at once into the sea, which is here of unknown depth.

sion on the minds of those men, whose habits are familiar with the most disgusting scenes of slaughter, that the utmost uneasiness is signified lest such a shocking purpose should be effected.

The heat of the sun reflected from the snow and ice, and also from the face of the rock, is intolerable; and

Numerous islands lie at various distances from each other, forming little bays and inlets. Horsehead, so called from some fancied resemblance, is one of these islands, beyond which is Hickson's Bay, which is very well sheltered and capacious, running very deep within the islands, and having a fine open entrance. Horsehead is the southern extremity of Hickson's Bay. The whale hunters give the name of Frow Islands to all the islands northward of the seventy-third degree; and to every recess, no matter how distinct from each other, they assign, in equal error, the name of Hickson's Bay; but the one now mentioned is that properly so called. This bay derives its name from the master of a ship, who was very successful in killing whales within it. They formerly resorted to this bay in great numbers; but from the repeated persecution of the whalers, they are seldom seen now in any continuance there. Sugar-Loaf Mountain appears very high over the islands on the north side of Hickson's Bay.* After passing the last mentioned bay, a string of islands irregularly elevated present themselves for a short distance, when a fine open and deep sound comes into view, with some peaked hills beyond its centre: delphinus leucas, larus maximus, terna hirundo, colymbus troile and grylle, procellaria glacialis.

Ice no longer in sight, save the immense bergs around, which mislead the eye by their resemblance to islands: at seven p. m. the wind again set in at N. E., fresh breeze; cirrostratus generally, but in the western region a stormy blue aggregation, which would portend a stiff wind from that quarter. The land at times

* There are some dangerous rocks near those islands, which should make the navigator cautious of entering the bay on the north side.

whilst on shore, though every step is almost knee-deep in the snow, the head and body are involved in a burning atmosphere.

Marshal's Bay, which we reached on the 27th of June, is, by the sweep which the current makes round its northern arm, a resting place for bergs,* where,

loaded with mist, but mostly clear to the eastward : on a sudden a mass of purplish brown cirrostratus arose on the horizon in W. S. W., and this was followed by a fine fresh breeze from the same point, when immediately the cloud of stormy blue assumed a creamy hue : at ten p. m. abreast of Sugar-Loaf Bay, which lies in latitude by observation 73° 50′ N. thirty-six ships in sight.

The islands forming the southern wing of Sugar-Loaf Bay are called the Seal Islands, from the great number of those animals formerly found there, from which haunt the frequent visits of the whale ships, and the persevering pursuit of the Uskee-mè have expelled them. The mountain which gives name to this bay is of a conical form, of which the above sketch gives an accurate view. This hill owes its distinguished elevation more to its standing alone, and to the flatness of the adjacent lands, than to its proper height. Four small islands lie near its base, which are a favourable retreat of the eider duck.

July 6 : ther. 32°, 42°, 40° : wind W. N. W., fresh breeze : weather thick with acicular snow collected into drops : the stormy blue cloud invariably portends a wind from the quarter wherein it appears, as is the case in the wind of this day which followed the

* A bay north of Jacob's Bay, and near Black Hook, is remarkably so, and thence is named Bergy Bay.

from their great weight, they fasten on the projecting rocks below, and unless moved by extraordinary increase of sea, from swells, or solution of inland ice, they are known to remain for years. Some of the sailors in the Thomas recognised in this bay two of several years' continuance, particularly a large ragged

indication of the preceding: the stormy blue cloud of yesterday, when observed, lay at a distance of about ten leagues: latitude observed at noon was 73° 42′ N.: a cumulostratus over the land to the eastward with accessory cumulus, which soon dispersed: land distant about eight leagues: in the afternoon passed the largest berg yet seen, more than 140 feet above the surface of the sea, and having a channelled summit like one already noticed: the body of this berg was riven into caverns, and its water edge was heaped with fragments like mountain debris; this was most observable on its north-eastern side, from which it would appear that a wind from that point had forced this mass through the islands, whilst in the straining these caverns were formed, the ruins of which were forced by the wind and waves back upon the berg in the manner just mentioned: throughout the afternoon the atmosphere continued clear and dry, yet somewhat chill from the presence of numerous straggling flaws: colymbus grylle and glocitans, procellaria glacialis and sterna hirundo.

At midnight the wind set in at S. W., light breeze, at which time a milky stratus encircled the horizon, and in the point of wind a beautiful exhibition of cirrocumulus occurred, the patches being edged with a rich tinting of sun-light, which contrasted with good effect to the purplish-brown swell of the centre. Out of this assemblage of small clouds, there issued a brilliant radiation of snow-white cirrus, such as has been observed in the journal on the 13th of June. This radiation seemed to shoot from behind and above the cirrocumulus cloud just mentioned, instantaneous, rapid, and resistless as the polar coruscation. At first a continuous stream of white issuing from an irregular coronal ring, apparently touching the cloud: from this ring a mazy spire descending held

berg more than two miles in extent. This is the one, which, when speaking of the arctic ice, I mentioned, as affording evidence of being rent from the continent above the Linnæan Isles. The lofty columnar tops with which it is crowned, are nothing but the ridges remaining of the icy mass, which has been channelled

communication with the cloud : from the point in which the sun was sweeping his lowest arch, other radiations, shorter and more sharp, came in response to the former, to which succeeded a gradual but uninterrupted change of the radiations from the cloud into a reticulated form with recurved points : the cirrocumulus also underwent a partial dissolution in the mean time ; the denser patches descending in loose yellowish-brown cirrostratus.

I have been thus particular in detailing the circumstances of this phenomenon, as I am not aware that the like has been before observed by any person else. Of its utility the philosophic reader may possibly form a better conclusion than I can presume to do ; yet as many such may not have the opportunity of witnessing the like, from the difficulty of access, whilst on the spot I felt it my duty, in the cause of science, to record what I had observed.

July 7 : ther. 42°, 46°, 32° : wind N. E., nearly calm : the radiation from S. W. still continues (10 a. m.) undiminished and very beautiful : in the zenith comoid cirrus, and purplish-brown cirrostratus suddenly forming in the horizon around : the weather delightfully fine : at noon the atmosphere became cloudless, the radiation having previously undergone a sudden solution into a milk-white hazy suffused state, and disappeared : the great berg last noticed not far distant : at one p. m. a single stream of cirrus sprung from S. W. appearing to embrace the opposite point of the horizon, at which moment I observed the thermometer at the degree noted as highest, and almost instantaneously a thick fog advanced from the northward.

At four p. m. the cirrus streamers increased in the same direction as the former, seeming to issue from an invisible corona in the S. W. under which lay a reddish-brown mist of cirrostratus.

by the annual torrents, that tumble from that extraordinary accumulation of congealed water. Neither does it require any of those "convulsions of nature," which sometimes shake the Andes, to cause such a separation of the above huge block from the enormous original. The simple visitation of the sun,

In the north-east point, at an elevation of about thirty degrees from the horizon, a similar mist, with circular base, appeared to be the source of corresponding streams of cirrus, which met the former in the zenith; and the meeting, or inosculation, as such a union has been called, was productive of cirrocumulus, which was immediately formed in flimsy patches: the cirrus streamers continued throughout this day fixed in nearly the direction of W. S. W. and E. N. E. which points correspond with the magnetical variation, observed on a meridian azimuth compass, by which I ascertained the variation to be somewhat beyond sixty-seven degrees north-west: latitude observed at noon 73° 46′ N. At midnight the radiation ceased, and the south-western region was darkly clouded, to which the rich sun-light of the hour afforded a pleasing contrast: at this hour the bursting of an ice berg rung upon the welkin for several minutes, with a report louder than that of the heaviest ordnance: thirty-two sail near: ship grappled in a flaw.

July 8: ther. 32°, 40°, 28°: wind N. E., fresh breeze: still anchored at the flaw, which shifts slowly to the southward; a strong tide current setting in that direction: at noon the tide flowed rapidly to the northward, causing numerous eddies along the edge of the flaw: the course of the current by compass was N. E. which, allowing for variation, is nearly N. N. W. more westerly: the whole sky during the forenoon was covered with broad irregular masses of cirrostratus of a light brown colour: the procellaria glacialis unusually active, which may be considered a certain indication of a strong wind; also the kittiwake appeared in great number, and was very clamorous. At four p. m. the masses of cumulostratus became confused into a uniform feature, varied only by a denser cloud of stormy blue, which lay sullen and still

every year, fails not to produce similar convulsions, and load the sea with ice bergs. But in the process of a few years, if such diminution continue, the supply must cease, and some future Danish historian will again have to "flee to the mountains" to ascertain the origin of others.

near the horizon in the N. E.: soon afterwards the wind grew strong and menacing: the ship was then set free of the flaw, as a situation near the ice is under such circumstances full of danger: up to the midnight hour it continued to blow a very strong gale, with a heavy sea.

July 9: ther. 33°, 34°, 32°: wind N. E., strong breeze: cirrostratus generally suffused over the sky, at times richly illuminated by the sun-light: numerous bergs around: procellaria glacialis, colymbus grylle, and Col. glocitans.

July 10: ther. 29°, 33°, 40°: wind N., nearly calm: atmosphere thick, and minute acicular snow falling: at noon more clear, when the snow ceased to fall, and the cloud became loose cirrostratus at a considerable elevation: a cumulostratus appeared in the eastward, where shortly afterwards land came into view; the presence of the latter cloud may be always considered as indicating land, and therefore the circumstance cannot be too strongly insisted on, and it is imperative on the navigator to know the form of this cloud well, and also to be aware of its indications; proper care in this respect may be a means of saving both the ship and seamen, or afford a gratifying anticipation of expected land. The remark refers specially to the appearance of the cumulostratus in Davis's Strait: ursus maritimus, colymbus glocitans, and larus eburneus; the latter very active and plunging in the sea, probably at the clio retusa, which appeared very numerous this day: wind at noon, soft light breeze at W.: afternoon the wind coming from S. W. with dark gray cirrostratus: to the northward, and close to the horizon, lay a broad belt of deep yellow intermixed with brown and red: this phenomenon is rare in Davis's Strait, but is frequent in the Spitzbergen seas: it is denomi-

Were the purposes of the voyage to allow advantage to be made of a short delay in Hickson's Bay, which we approached on the 5th of July, a very valuable acquisition might be obtained of eider down; the ducks of that species frequenting the low islands on the north side in countless numbers, for the pur-

nated field blink, being present wherever a continuous tract of bergy ice occurs.

July 11 : ther. 32°, 40°, 33° : wind N. by W., light breeze : cirrostratus grayish-brown, thinly diffused, which as it passes over the zenith admits of a view : cirrus and cirrocumulus at a vast height above, apparently in the most tranquil state. The water is intensely blue : at noon a well-marked nimbus appeared advancing from the northward : latitude observed 74° 42′ N. : the yellow blink still visible : the sun-light passing through the denser parts of the cirrostratus in the south-west, the cloud in places became intensely bright, and very painful to the sight, so that the eye would be less distressed gazing on the luminary itself : procellaria glacialis, colymbus glocitans and troile, larus eburneus.

July 12 : ther. 33°, 40°, 28° : wind variable, at times calm : cirrostratus generally diffused : some whales seen ; also a monodon monoceros of great size : two groups of seals in emigration passed to the northward : numerous flocks of colymbus glocitans at a very great elevation passing in the same direction : at noon the zenith clearing : extensive cirrocumulus of snowy whiteness appeared above : at the same time a berg, not far distant, burst with a noise resembling thunder, which continued heavy and long in reiteration over the ice : an immense flaw is descending rapidly from the northward : larus maximus and eburneus, colymbus grylle, P. glacialis.

July 13 : ther. 30°, 49°, 32° : wind N., light and variable : the sun obscured with grayish cirrostratus : the weather delightfully fine : a female whale killed : the longest lamina (whalebone) measured nine feet ten inches : clio retusa, and many species of medusa, are very numerous in these waters : at ten a. m.

pose of rearing their young. As the care of the parent bird is so great, that it will devest itself of its own soft covering to guard its young against the inclemency of the climate, the nest may, to such as seek it, afford a good supply of that very valuable material; one island alone, as I have been correctly informed,

the wind changed to W. S. W., light breeze: soon after the thermometer indicated forty-nine, when the glass was covered with condensed vapour in drops: cirrocumulus in snowy exhibition decorated the zenith: latitude observed at noon 74° 45′ N.: at this time the wind came from the southward, fresh breeze: many flaws of ice around.

July 14: ther. 32°, 38°, 30°: wind N. E., strong breeze: weather clear, with cirrocumulus at a great elevation, and cirrostratus in profile in the south: at ten a. m. the clouds showed signs of land, and at noon the summits of four islands came in sight: at this hour a beautiful display of cirrus radiation * occurred, darting through the cirrocumulus field, which underwent instantaneous dissolution: colymbus glocitans in numerous flocks, enlivening the dreary scene with its busy bustling flight and cheerful notes: a fog indicated by a light gray stratus in N. and W.

July 15: ther. 36°, 42°, 34°: wind N., light breeze.

July 16: ther. 36°, 48°, 38°: wind N. E., light breeze: the ship advancing towards land on a S. E. course, came in with an extensive field of ice reaching to the Linnæan Isles: this field was interspersed with numerous bergs, and appeared unbroken for leagues in extent, east and west.

The state of cloud this day, beautiful cirrocumulus, and flimsy comoid cirrus, the points of which were scattered in every direction: the atmosphere to the northward unclouded, and sky of a pearly blue hue: a pair of burgomasters on wing: colymbus grylle and colymbus glocitans in associated and numerous flocks: several of the monodon monoceros came from under the field of

* Corresponding with the magnetic variation very exactly.

furnishing several pounds of down. Besides, the old birds are so anxious for the safety of their progeny as to be regardless of their own, so that they are made an easy spoil to the marksman. The skins of the anas mollissima, as I have before noticed, are in very high estimation.

ice, or played along its edge, and numerous families of seals were observed in merry emigration passing to the westward.

July 17: ther. 38°, 52°, 38°: wind N. E., fresh breeze: not a speck of cloud to be seen: the air unusually hot: the continent of ice distinctly seen: latitude observed at noon 75° 17′ N.: larus maximus and delphinus leucas in great number: colymbus glocitans in large flocks, sometimes flying very high: an odd colymbus troile appeared; and col. grylle in parties of five: few seals seen.

July 18: ther. 48°, 42°, 32°: wind N. E., light air: the state of atmosphere still the same, and not a speck of cloud to be seen: at noon a bright fog bank arose in the south-west, which afterward extended itself over the whole sky, verifying the assertion, that it is observed to move against the wind: a procellaria glacialis appeared entirely white: larus maximus and eburneus: the monodon appeared in great number this day, and the Thomas's men succeeded in killing one male and two females: the latter were destitute of the tooth: they are always taken without that instrument, which is solely conferred on the male either for ornament or annoyance: the male monodon measured from snout to tail fourteen feet: the horn six feet eight inches: there was also a minute one in the left socket, but not projecting beyond the skin: three finners passed near the ship; they seemed about forty feet in length each: a female whale (balæna mysticetus) killed this day, measured sixty feet: it received the harpoon but once, and dived away under the ice, drawing down three boats' lines, being 1080 fathoms, and died at the bottom: immense groups of the oniscus ceti attached to the under lip, and to the under part of the fins: the edge of the fleshy covering, embracing

Several ships killed whales during the 13th of July, those animals having appeared in greater number than usual, generally in groups of five and six together. It is, as formerly noticed, in such circumstances extremely dangerous to strike one of the group, as the others, in the confusion of escape, make such irregular and

the root of the monodon's tooth, was covered with insects of the same description : it appeared somewhat singular that not a mallemuck, with the exception of the white one above noticed, came near the ship this day, though the men were engaged flinching, until the latter part, when a few appeared, which were evidently new comers, as was remarked by their clean feathers and voracious efforts : the fog continued throughout, leaving the zenith unusually clear : a luminous arch appeared this afternoon in opposition to the sun, but destitute of iridescence : the whole interior of this arch was strongly luminous, and objects within its compass partook of that illumination : I thought it worthy of a place among the sketches, as not having been heretofore noticed in any publication within my experience : the sun-light at midnight is strong to an intense degree ; but, owing probably to the presence of the ice, the thermometer stands at 32° : the water here is brownish green, and abounds with the clio retusa, and many species of medusa.

July 19 : ther. 42°, 46°, 34° : wind S. E., light breeze : at an early hour this day, the fog had entirely dispersed, and no cloud appeared, except a yellow stratus : the field blink, in the horizon all around : the sun-light in this stratus has a most distressing effect on the eyes, causing very painful inflammation, and scorching the face in an incredible degree : the ship remained stationed near the field of ice in company with ten others, all engaged in the look-out for whales : the water throughout this day was smooth as glass, except where ruffled by the colymbus glocitans diving after the flimsy, artless clio, which seems to be the favourite food of the roch : numerous individuals of the larus maximus appeared ; also L. eburneus in great flocks : procellaria glacialis and colymbus

violent motions, that any boat within reach of them is apt to be destroyed: many such accidents occurred within view, but fortunately no life was lost. The movements of the whale are truly terrible when writhing in the agonies of wound; and when the deadly barb is plunged into his body, his harmless nature di-

grylle, the latter observed to be in pairs: the Linnæan Isles at midnight still in view, distant about seven leagues: many ships, five particularly, are at the same time dangerously circumstanced amongst packed ice to the westward.

July 20: ther. 45°, 52°, 48°: wind N. E., light breeze: ship stationed nearly as the preceding day: those ships which were to the westward succeeded in getting clear from the ice, which otherwise would have inevitably crushed them to pieces: the object of the masters, in going so far in that direction, was to intercept the whale in his progress east and west: and in this respect not one of them had success, the ships which remained the most to eastward having killed a good many.

Latitude observed at noon 75° 8′ N.: larus eburneus, and colymbus glocitans, few throughout this day: procellaria glacialis also few in number: it would seem as if these birds had proceeded to the southward warned by the indications of the season, which, to human observation, are not so discernible as to those migratory animals. From the great number of the monodon monoceros seen and killed in view of the Linnæan Isles, I have marked the place upon the chart "Unicorn Bay." At eight p. m. some very light cirrus appeared in the zenith, and towards S. E.: larus maximus and colymbus grylle came into view frequently in the course of the evening: the water in Unicorn Bay is of the colour of the bay-leaf, and crowded with mollusca: the tide setting strongly, as heretofore, observed north and south by compass: at a later hour the cirrus changed into cirrocumulus, evidently communicating with loose patches of cirrostratus lower down: ship laid to by the flaw, as on the 17th current.

July 21: ther. 34°, 48°, 42°: wind, a perfect calm: at three

rects the monster only to escape. If ever struck before, memory, and the dread of such another attack, exci alarm at the presence of a boat, when the flurry i vhich the animal endeavours to make off is attended with extreme danger to the pursuer, particularly if a number happen to be in company when one is

a. m. this morning a most magnificent display of radiation occurred, of which a sketch has been attempted. The cirrus radiation here remarked is always observed to issue from a body of detached clouds, assuming the form of an arch. Whether this curved arrangement be actually in a portion of the circumference of a circle, or merely an optical delusion, I will not undertake to assert, but the curve invariably appeared to me arched, as I have related: the basis arch of the phenomenon which occurred this morning was of amazing span, embracing several leagues of sea, the central radius passing through the horizon in nearly E. by N. per compass; which corresponds closely with the point of variation. The radiation darted rapidly and irregularly towards the opposite point of the sky, in pale white spires. The atmosphere in the southern region immediately became suffused with whitish brown cirrostratus. Soon afterwards various beautiful changes to minute cirrocumulus and comoid cirrus were observable. Within the arch lay a long linear bed of cirrostratus, almost black, which preserved a horizontal position and unaltered form during the radiation and the changes mentioned. In the space of three hours from the first appearance, the whole was dissolved and dissipated, leaving the atmosphere free of visible cloud, but not quite clear, being of a milky blue. I should not have intruded upon the reader's notice the detail of this radiation, had I not been convinced, by repeated observations, that there exists a close, it may be said a direct, correspondence between its appearance and the variation of the needle. From what cause this singular coincidence proceeds, it will still longer I fear remain to be explored. The facts, however, which are herein exhibited, may be relied on for the accuracy and faithfulness of report, and may induce some enlightened

struck, the fugitives being then most dangerous. A pair also engaged in the dalliance of nature are dangerous to be approached, as happened in the case of the one above mentioned being killed: her companion at the same time being struck, both wounded descended to the bottom, and rose again to seek each

and able mind to study a satisfactory illustration of the phenomenon. It is right also to inform the reader, that during the formation and continuance of the radiation, no irregular motion of the compass was observable; the entire process appearing to go on at an elevation far too great to admit of any influence on the needle. The state of cloud, its being invariably a base of distinct cirrostratus in a curved chain, the radiation always issuing as it would appear from behind the cirrostratus, and having a cirrus consistence, and all those appearances being usually succeeded by a wind from the opposite point, besides the correspondence with the variation, are circumstances well worthy of the philosopher's attention. At noon the sky became free of every speck of cloud, when a light breeze from the W. by S. carried the ship slowly to the eastward: light cirrus formed: latitude observed 75° 12′ N.

July 22: ther. 33°, 38°, 34°: wind very variable: from midnight the wind blew furiously from S. W. a strong gale; changed at noon to N. W. light air with fog: about six p. m. a light breeze from W. converted the fog into light rain: in the evening later the wind became very variable, inclining to northward, with rain: at ten p. m. the wind coming to N. E., the upper atmosphere cleared, and exhibited cirrocumulus: no birds to be seen, but an odd mallemuck going southward.

The state of this day is full of those indications that mark the necessity of ships proceeding to the southward, about this date, and even sooner. The Thomas was the last ship that moved off; the rest of the fleet, except a few, having some days since departed. The greatest apprehension of danger arises from the presence of fog, in which, if a vessel become involved, and carried by the current among the packed ice and bergs, there is little chance of

other, when a boat belonging to the ship which struck the male whale was dashed to pieces by a jerk of the tail: the men were however saved by a boat which happened to be near. The female died at the bottom, and, on being hauled up with the line, the under jaw was covered with yellow mud.

The weather during the early part of the 15th of July, equalled in fineness that experienced in the temperate latitudes at the same date, the sun-light being exceedingly strong: a slight mist came on just before noon, but soon cleared away. The ship laid to near the flaw edge, afforded a very distinct view of the islands, which, as the accounts of the most experienced navigators inform me, have not been seen before. I therefore presume to give them the name of the Linnæan Isles, in honour of the prince of natural historians.

The atmosphere, at noon, being obscured by a fog,

avoiding destruction: neither can the utmost vigilance guard against such a visitation. The winds being now, usually, very variable, the state of the weather may in the course of an hour change from clear and fine to that of the thickest fog.

July 23: ther. 34°, 44°, 38°: wind E., light breeze: from the midnight hour the breeze continued steady till noon, freshening a good deal in the early part of the day: cirrostratus in every species covering the sky: at a little before noon, the whole cloud passed into general suffusion very rapidly, and became very attenuated: at noon a splendidly white fog bank lay immensely along the land in the north-east, the low tops being then just visible above the horizon: the fog bank came onwards, slow but unimpeded in progress, involving all the lower objects in interminable obscurity, and shutting up an elegant display of cirrocumulus, resting apparently on cirrostratous beds, which had previously formed in an elevated position.

which advanced from the eastward, presented an observation. The mist in the afternoon appearing rather shallow, the upper atmosphere being mostly clear, I was induced to ascend to the hurricane house, in hopes of seeing the land more satisfactorily, when a phenomenon of novel character presented itself to view.

The sun-light falling on the mist formed an ellipsis strongly illuminated, apparently rising from the surface of the sea to the upper edge of the mist, at an angle of about twenty degrees from the horizon. In this ellipsis the iridescent colours were not distinguishable. The inner edge was pearly white, with the faintest tinge of blue; the middle yellowish, deepening into brown and purple; the outer edge a blackish blue; beyond that, a brighter line; outside of which again lay the cirrostratus mist in its peculiar brown. Within, the ellipsis was bounded by a deep blue line, and the inner space filled with mist of the same colour and illumination as the exterior.

In one centre of the ellipsis my shadow appeared depicted, the head surrounded with a circle of the liveliest iridescence. Beyond this was another with similar iridescence; but the colours were reversed in order, and more faint; the belts were also broader. One circumstance surprised me much: whilst the ellipsis rose at an angle from the horizon, the iris circle appeared depicted on the surface of the sea. No account of such a phenomenon having in my recollection been recorded, I thought it might be deemed worthy of consideration.

The Linnæan Islands run in a curve, bending westward and northward, from the Greenland side across Davis's Straits, and by their resistance prevent the descent of that amazing accumulation of ice to which the name of icy continent is given. In the open spaces between the islands, the ice continent appears abruptly broken, as if large bergs had been detached in former years. There is also a sloping debris at the bottom similar to rock. The upper surface of the continent is torn in diverging channels, evidently worn successfully every summer by the dissolved snow. The great body of the polar ice rises as it extends northward; and where it leans against the islands, it, in many places, out-tops them. The channels on this icy continent all, so far as they were visible, were directed southerly. Through the spaces between the islands, the bergs obtain a passage, and coming in contact with the rock, either when forced from their original situation, or in their passage, they are frequently stained a brown colour. This the sailors call black ice. The general appearance of the Linnæan Isles is bare basaltic or floetz trap rock. They are in general small, two only being about ten or twelve miles in length. From my chart, which was made with the utmost accuracy, the number of these islands is eighty, lying at irregular but short distances from each other. One of the largest of the Linnæan Isles lies to the northward of the chain in the western extremity, and is of a conical form, much more elevated than the others, and is covered with snow. Many smaller islands lie grouped around, as well as to the southward of it, and at a very short distance from each other. This island is easily discoverable on the chart from its superior extent.

The latitude of the next larger island to the southward was found, by observation, to be 75° 3′ N.; and the variation determined the same time, by an azimuth compass, and corrected to the time at Greenwich, was exactly 82¼°.

On the 16th, ten whales were remarked invariably running eastward and westward, out from the Greenland waters, and others again pursuing a contrary course. The whale hunters are so convinced of this, that they sail always in that direction when in high latitudes. Hence the obvious conclusion must be, that the further emigration of those animals northward is limited to the Linnæan Isles; and that too, from the impossibility of their obtaining a supply of air underneath the icy continent. Indeed, when a whale is struck, if it happen to run for the ice, the hunters are almost certain of its capture, as it must come out again for breath, when the boats, being arranged along the edge of the field, are sure to be ready to repeat the blow the instant the animal reappears. I saw one, which was so wounded, succeed in spying out a small hole within that ice field, where scarcely more than the head had access to the air; and there the creature rose in imagined security, at a great distance from the edge; but the blowing soon exposed his situation, both from the sound, and the watery column driven up in respiration; and the hunters having pursued across the ice to the spot, soon succeeded in despatching their victim.

Among the whales, on the 20th, taken, there was a

young one, about half grown; and as this circumstance is rare in Davis's Strait, though frequently occurring in the seas around Spitzbergen, it would strongly support the opinion that Greenland is terminable at a very low degree from the pole; nor would this presumption be misapplied if extended to the American continent, which reaches little, if at all, further northward than the latitude of the Linnæan Isles. In this sweep of the arctic region, some promontory may hereafter be found to violate the line such as Spitzbergen does; but the fact of no land lying around the pole may be fairly presumed; and of this fact I have to adduce a weighty proof from the observations communicated by one of the masters who proceeded so far to the westward, being one of the five yesterday in danger.

"After clearing the ice, all to the northwest was heavy open sea, the swell and current coming from that point, and no obstruction appeared against proceeding as far north as he pleased: at all events, a hundred miles further (more than three degrees) were accessible." But as open sea presents little chance of meeting with the whale, in a state of rest, this person, mindful of his oath, deemed it adviseable to return to the eastward. This part of the Journal will be useful in reference to our inquiry, when further considering the subject of the northwest passage.

A lofty berg this day came in view, with a Gothic arch, at least 100 feet high, passing quite through one extremity; the bottom of the arch was covered with the fragments that had fallen from the cavity above. Over the crown of this arch, a broad and heavy superstructure of the icy mass sat suspended, offering an appearance of stability awfully deceptive; under which, were an antiquarian to stand taking a drawing from this extraordinary structure, very few persons of common caution would venture to ensure his life: the washing of the sea had worn a bay within the bosom of this berg, which bore strongly the semblance of land, and the ruins of the icy arch added forcibly to the deception.

From the remarks in the preceding day's journal (to which the reader is referred) the approach of the fog bank, on the 23d of July, must have been contemplated with much uneasiness. At a distance from the land, which at best could only relieve from the apprehension of drowning; in a latitude which forbade every hope of escape or prolonged life, were the ship to founder; and well aware that the all-involving fog would have its ruinous effects increased by any degree of breeze; it may not be exaggeration to say, that such a situation could by no means be considered enviable. *Having advanced further north than the whalers* (who are certainly most intrepid and daring navigators) *had ever ventured before;* the circumstance also of the Thomas being the last to return, though some others were in sight; and the apprehension that the wind coming from the southward, or westward of south, might set the yet undissolved ice again towards the inhospitable shores of Greenland, and so preclude the possibility of return, were matters for reflection little calculated to preclude alarm. Under those circumstances, however, the discipline of the men, however rude it may be considered, kept every mind on the alert; and the ship's forecastle and bow were never without a careful eye to look out for danger. As the fog advanced in the afternoon, the whole surrounding scene became obscured; many bergs had been previously seen, and the necessary precautions had been vigilantly insisted on. Notwithstanding all the care of the watch on deck, the ship came unexpectedly within half her bowsprit-length of a frowning berg, deeply cloaked with mist, which, in the temperature of the hour, it was throwing off in clouds, and was of course in such a tendency to solution, that the least touch from any part of the ship would have produced a disruption capable of overwhelming her in an instant. Fortunately, by backing the sails immediately, the danger was avoided; and other vessels, four in number, coming on the same course in succession, were, by the cries of the men from the other ships, successively warned of the situation. Many heavy flaws lay around, offering such openings to the eastward as were at first thought to lead to open water; but hope to that effect was found deceptive, and the ships were compelled to warp back again to the westward, to get clear of the flaws.

The sea in this latitude, which is that of Devil's Thumb, must be shallow, as an innumerable hoard of bergs is hereabouts remarkable, though the current to the southward is still strong enough to set them in that direction. From the summits of those bergs an accumulation of vapour, exuded under the influence of the sun, assumes a form similar to a cumulous cloud, or, as some readers may more familiarly represent it to their recollection—such an appearance as, on a greater scale, caps the mountains' summit in temperate climes, before or after rainy weather. The various fantastic forms of those bergs adds to this imaginary representation; many not a hundred feet in elevation, seeming to be mountains in miniature surrounded with appropriate exhalations; and others, from their sharp squared summits, would afford a picture, not absurdly alike, of palaces whose many summits, by the streaming smoke, gave indication of the luxury within.

In the afternoon the fog cleared away, and gave to the view several islands, towards and along which the ship was running under a fresh breeze N. by E.

At the termination of this coast, and at a considerable distance N. E. of the most northern island in the line, stands that singular rock which the sailors denominate the Devil's Thumb, being an isolated rock, standing, as it were, the goal of northern voyage in Davis's Strait.

To the south-westward of the Devil's Thumb is a large, long, rugged island, which is the most northwesterly of Greenland in those seas, covering the waters in which is seated the Devil's Thumb to the north-east, and sufficiently distinct in distance to be considered not a part of the chain of the Linnæan Isles. Within the above-mentioned large island lies an extensive sound of unknown bounds eastward, and which to the southward is terminated by the islands forming the northern extremity of Sugar-loaf Bay. Numerous other islands lie to the westward of the above sound, but imperfectly known from the casual visits of the whale hunters, who only know those lands when shut in by the ice descending from the northward, where they remain until the sea becomes sufficiently safe for their purpose. Under such circumstances, the masters of the whale ships only know the land as it may afford them an hour's shooting, with their rusty fowling pieces, in order to bring home some eider duck skins to the wives of their acquaintance, or the friends of their employers. Yet even here there is population, perhaps endeared by domestic sweets. This thought recalls the picture so admirably drawn by Horace, who could have scarcely imagined that his delightful words would so happily suit the situation. With the indulgence of the reader I shall venture to apply them to this, as I believe, the last retreat of social human life.

Pone me, pigris ubi nulla campis
Arbor æstivâ recreatur aura:
Quod latus mundi, nebulæ, malusque
Jupiter urget.
Pone sub curru nimiùm propinqui
Solis, in terra domibus negata,
Dulce ridentem Lalagen amabo,
Dulce loquentem.

Place me, where frost the most severe
Forbids the tree a summer's air,
In fogs oppressed and sad—
Where wheels the sun's eternal course,
Still teeming light with boundless force,
Nor human eye is glad;
There give me but the honeyed smile,
And those sweet sounds which care beguile,
There Lalagé, and life!

To many readers, I fear, the foregoing detail of views in the most northerly parts of Davis's Strait may appear tedious and unsatisfactory. To such I would presume to say, that a faithful account of any part of the globe, which has been hitherto imperfectly described, cannot be destitute of interest, though the subject, as in the present instance, be of the lowliest and most barren description in ordinary view. To another class of readers I would address a loftier appeal. To such minds as seek a knowledge of the actual state of the earth, beyond the pale of vegetation, where nature slumbers in eternal lethargy, and is roused into feverish motion only for a very short portion of the summer months, under the influence of a perpetual sun; to such readers, I say, a view of those regions, drawn by a person earnest in the cause of science, and anxious to behold the effects of correct opinion propagated, must be of some value. Under these considerations I have ventured to exhibit those scenes, in order that the reader, who possesses only a wish to indulge cursory opinion, as well as the more deeply reflecting reader, may both find entertainment. The former, by indulging that propensity to curiosity which forms the ground of much of the happiness of life, may, in perusing the particulars of this excursion, meet occasionally with some agreeable circumstance amidst the dreary and desolate picture of an icy region, which, for seven months in each year, is shut from access by continual frost. To know from what causes a variety of the human species cherishes an abode in such inhospitable climes, with an enthusiastic attachment to such deserts, and why any portion of mankind would suffer that predilection to forbid removal to more genial latitudes, forms alone a topic for consideration of much interest. The migration of birds and other animals to high northern latitudes, their habits and pursuits in such situations as they frequent, their periods of return southward, or emigration in other directions, furnish the mind with store for valuable reflection. All these points are comprised, and recorded as they occurred, in the Journal just submitted to the notice of the reader.

The latter description of reader has now laid before him for investigation a mass of facts in natural history, important in many points of view. To philosophic research I leave such inquiry, and the useful application of the results, in the hope that, from the heap, some deduction may be drawn of importance in the concerns of science and of mankind. Neither am I, in this regard, actuated by a desire to arrogate to myself any merit for furnishing those facts. It was my good fortune to find that the motives which urged me into those high latitudes were rewarded by having presented to my view many appearances in nature which were quite new to my observation; and if they appear so to others, and prove of any benefit to society, my gratification will be multiplied.

Some atmospheric phenomena, such for instance as are recorded in the preceding Journal, have not, in the extent of my reading, come previously within my knowledge; and particularly that of the cirrus radiation, which bears a correspondence with the magnetic variation; if any of my readers consider with me, that these are new in description, and that they can furnish any useful results, then I shall not consider my time and anxiety thrown away.

In this pursuit I went unbidden and unsolicited; and should my inquiries, as I trust they will, afford either entertainment or profit to the general or philosophic reader, I shall consider such approbation a proper stimulus to contribute my humble mite, on every fit occasion, in aid of the cause of science.

In giving publication also to the result of my inquiries in the arctic seas, I have to boast of a loftier motive: viz. the deep concern I feel in the cause of humanity. Having learned lately that an expedition is preparing to set out for those seas, with intent to explore a north-westerly passage, by a polar route, into the North Pacific Ocean, I should deem myself culpable in withholding from the public at large, as well as from the projectors of that undertaking, such particulars of the natural state of the higher northern latitudes, as I had, during the course of last summer, a full opportunity of observing.

With that view, therefore, I drew the reader's attention to the actual state of those countries during the summer months, when only the arctic waters are navigable; and, in the course of the Journal, a faithful and accurate account of almost every hour's state of weather, wind and water is recorded.

Those circumstances I have laid down as a basis for some observations, which I shall take an opportunity of submitting on the subject; which, from its importance, is worthy of the most serious consideration, not only as it regards the safety of the individuals engaged in the expedition, but as involving in its results matter of the weightiest interest to the trade and general commerce of Great Britain.

The importance of this subject has long since attracted the attention of the autocrat of all the Russias, whose government, doubtlessly envious of the preponderance of the power of Great Britain upon the ocean, seeks the most active and effectual means of anticipating her research to countries hitherto unexplored by Europeans.

It is well known that the Emperor Alexander has at this moment some vessels, under the command of Lieut. Kotzebue, who, having examined the islands in the northern Pacific, between Kamtschatka and the North American shores, is waiting in some station near Behring's Strait, for the opening of the ice in the ensuing spring, in order to push his researches, if possible, across the polar seas into Davis's Strait, or directly forwards, should circumstances favour an enterprise of such adventurous daring, and reach by such attempt some port in the north of Russia.

As this curious subject has long engaged public attention, it may not be improper in this place to take a cursory view of the attempts hitherto made to discover a passage westward into the Pacific. The account shall be as brief as possible.

CHAPTER VII.

OF THE ATTEMPTS WHICH HAVE BEEN MADE TO DISCOVER A NORTH-WEST PASSAGE.

So early, it appears, was this subject of navigating the arctic seas entertained, with an expectation of obtaining an intercourse with India in that direction, east or west, that in the year 901, Alfred the Great is said to have engaged a mariner named Other, a native of Heligoland, to survey the coasts of Norway and Lapland, and to discover if any opening in a north-east direction would admit of a passage to India on that side. The navigator above mentioned, on his return, gave the monarch an account of the Norwegian and Lapland countries, and of the inhabitants, who subsisted by fishing and killing whales. A subsequent inquiry during the reign of the same prince confirmed the accuracy of Other's account.

In the year 1497, John Cabot, a native of Venice, fired with a desire to imitate the example of Columbus, and encouraged by the merchants of Bristol, where he then resided, made an application to the King (Henry VII.) to be permitted to make a voyage of discovery across the Atlantic Ocean. His request was readily complied with, and letters patent furnished him, but enjoining strictly a return to the port of Bristol. That enterprising navigator accordingly set sail; and he appears to have been the original projector of the north-west passage, after the example of Columbus, who, in a similar attempt at a southern latitude, had made his grand discovery of America.

Cabot, inferring from the accounts of Columbus, that a probability might exist of the ocean being open to the northward, directed his course to the north-westward in this expectation; and on the 24th of June discovered Newfoundland, which he named Prima Vista or First-seen-land. Still actuated by his original intention, he sailed further to the northward, and discovered Cape Florida, where he found people already established, answering exactly to the description of the Uskee-mès. From this place he returned to England, carrying with him three of the natives, as a proof of success. Such an act, however, could not tend to impress that simple and harmless people with amicable feelings towards their visiters.

In 1521, the fame of Cabot's expedition encouraged some French merchants to send out a countryman of their own, named Jaques Cartier, to discover a north-west passage to the East-Indies; but it seems he penetrated no further than the Bay of St. Lawrence, and, otherwise unsuccessful, he returned home the same year.

In the year 1536, the origin of the fishery on the banks of Newfoundland arose from a voyage made from Bristol, by Mr. Robert Thorne, a merchant of that place, who, with the King's permission, which on such occasion appeared indispensable, fitted out a ship at his own expense, and sailed to Newfoundland

and Cape Breton, discovering the very valuable fishery of Newfoundland on his passage. By the discovery of Thorne, the naval and commercial prosperity of England has been in a great degree promoted, the fishery, from its justly estimated importance, having down to the present day been firmly maintained in British monopoly. Thorne made this great discovery merely by accident, as his purpose on setting sail was also to ascertain the possibility of a north-west passage.

In the last year of Edward VI. and whilst that promising young prince was confined to his death-bed by sickness, an expedition was planned, under the command of Sir Hugh Willoughby, to prosecute a voyage to China by the north-east passage, if such could be ascertained. For this purpose three ships were fitted out; but from the obstruction of the ice, though the ships set out in May 20, 1553, Sir Hugh could advance only to the seventy-second degree, and was there shut in, and obliged to winter in Russian Lapland, where that intrepid adventurer and his crew most miserably perished, in consequence of the excessive cold. One of the ships engaged in this unfortunate expedition was more successful in getting through the ice, under the command of Capt. Chancellor, who passed the North Cape to the eastward, and got safely into the bay of St. Nicholas on the Russian coast, being the first European that had conducted a ship into those waters.

At the representations of Capt. Carleton, upon his return, the whale fishery was undertaken, and several ships were subsequently fitted out in that trade, which afterwards led to the discovery of Spitzbergen.

In 1556, Capt. Stephen Burrough, promising himself better success than was experienced in the unhappy voyage of Sir Hugh Willoughby, ventured upon a similar expedition; but his attempt to discover a north-east passage was unavailing.

Sir Martin Frobisher, in the year 1567, under the auspices of Queen Elizabeth, undertook to ascertain the existence of a north-west passage. The Earl of Warwick, in a spirit of patriotism, encouraged Capt. Frobisher warmly in this undertaking, and in consequence he sailed in June with two barks and a pinnace. In this voyage the east coast of Greenland was seen in latitude 63° 8′ N. He here discovered the strait, which he called after his own name. Here also he lost five of his men whom he set on shore; and by a very unwise and unfair retaliation he seized upon one of the natives, and carried him away to England. That such proceeding was unjustifiable is evident from his being at the time in a state of uncertainty about the fate of his own men, whose lives, if spared by the natives up to the time in which the Uskee-mè was seized, might probably have been preserved, but such a proceeding could only produce the worst consequences.

Captain Frobisher brought home in this voyage a piece of stone of a black colour, which some chemists of that day pronounced to contain gold; and this event tended to recommend another expedition to the same place in quest of that precious ore. High expectations were entertained that a most valuable discovery had been made on that occasion.

Accordingly, by the exertions of his patron, the Earl of Warwick, he was despatched in 1577 in quest of the land of gold; and the better to secure success, he was provided with one of her Majesty's ships, attended by the two barks. He again saw the land lying at the entrance of the strait, and called it Queen Elizabeth's Foreland. Having sent ashore to make strict search after his men, which proved he was doubtful of their fate, all inquiry was ineffectual, and he hesitated not to carry off two men and one woman prisoners. Here he took on board a quantity of the ore, which afterwards, being carefully examined, turned out altogether worthless. The Queen was so much pleased with the account given of this voyage, that she called the supposed continent Meta Incognita.

In 1578, her Majesty ordered a grand expedition under the same commander. The fleet consisted of fifteen sail, carrying a colony of 120 persons, who were to be left in the newly-discovered country, with three ships for their use. Materials of wood for building habitations for the colonists were provided along with other suitable supplies; but a storm having overtaken the squadron, the ship carrying the materials for building foundered, and the undertaking so grandly begun ended in nothing; the fleet not having even been able to find the strait.

Captain Frobisher was afterwards advanced to the honour of knighthood for the bravery with which he contributed to the destruction of the Spanish armada in 1588.

In the year 1580, the Russia Company fitted out two ships for the discovery of a north-east passage. That undertaking proved unsuccessful and unfortunate, one of the ships having been lost, and all on board perished.

In 1585, the hope of finding the so much desired north-west passage induced Mr. John Davis to undertake it, though so many previous attempts had failed. He took the precaution to avail himself of the experience of Mr. Fenton, who had been engaged in former voyages for the same purpose. Davis set sail on the 7th of June, and, on the 20th of July following, discovered the Island of Desolation on the west coast of Greenland, where he found the natives a civil, tractable, and honest people. Having proceeded further to the northward, he discovered the strait which has been since called after his name. Steering west, he came in sight of the land on the American side of the strait, and called the lofty mountains which he there observed Mount Raleigh.

In his second voyage, in 1586, Capt. Davis advanced to latitude 60° 47′ N. where he again saw land, but met much obstruction from the ice, which he avoided by running to the westward, and afterwards succeeded in reaching the 54° 15′ of latitude, where he also found an inoffensive people. The land here appeared broken, with great sounds and inlets.

Captain Davis was again sent out in the following year, when he penetrated to lat. 72° 12′ N. where he discovered a great many islands; and from the number of women who were there, he named them the Women's or Frow Islands. A remarkable promontory here he called Hope Sanderson. This was the greatest distance to the northward that Davis ever reached. Steering westward from Hope Sanderson, he ran a distance of forty leagues, and again fell in with Mount Raleigh. Davis, to the last, remained confident of the practicability of a north-west passage.

After the failure of Davis's attempt, all expeditions in search of a north-west passage were for some years suspended; but the public mind in the interval was busily occupied with numerous pamphlets, and other publications, both for and against the possible execution of such a design.

In 1602, Captain George Weymouth made another effort, but with singular want of success. His attempt was not calculated to support the arguments of those who were in favour of the measure, and it was again abandoned.

The intrepid, but unfortunate Hudson, next took up the subject, imagining that, by exploring the seas to the northward of Spitzbergen, he might have a better chance of success, by sailing towards the North Pole in that direction.

With this view, in 1607, he sailed northward, and in latitude 73° 12′ he saw the land of Spitzbergen. He there observed the elevation of the sun at midnight to be 10° 40′ above the horizon: in this voyage Captain Hudson penetrated to 82° nearly, and thought to effect his passage to N. W. that way; but an impenetrable barrier of ice forbade further progress.

In the year 1608 he again renewed his efforts in the same sea, where he met with much difficulty from the ice; he then tried a N. E. passage, but without effect. Another endeavour was made by the same persevering individual in 1609 in the same quarter; but this ended as fruitless as the former.

Defeat seemed to spur his exertions, and the following year he set sail across the Atlantic, big with expectation, which was increased by his discovery of the strait and bay, on the North American side, which have been meritedly called after this indefatigable navigator. After having traversed much of that bay, Captain Hudson, a man of ardent mind, felt himself still not satisfied, and intimated an intention of looking out for some situation in which himself and his men might continue in safety during the winter, but when the provision, which had been laid in only for six months' consumption, came to be examined, the stock was found nearly exhausted.

Hudson melting into tears on observing the unhappy situation of his people, distributed all the biscuit among them, and this inconsiderate act of generosity was cruelly repaid by a mutiny. An ungrateful wretch named Green, to whom the Captain had been remarkably indulgent, having conspired with the mate of the ship, and the majority of the crew, sent the unfortunate man with his son, a youth, a Mr. Woodhouse, who was an eminent mathematician, and five of the hands who remained faithful to their master, all adrift in the shallop.

Those unhappy persons undoubtedly soon perished in that dreary region, as no account of them was ever after obtained. The ruffianly crew, with much difficulty, and in the greatest hardship, endeavoured to return home, and one only of the wretches survived their attempt to recount the melancholy tale. Thus terminated the efforts of the unhappy Hudson, a man in every respect worthy of a better fate.

Captain Button was afterwards sent out in the year 1612, in hopes of recovering poor Hudson; and after encountering great dangers in Hudson's Bay and Strait, having been, on one occasion, intercepted in the Strait by the ice, he lay with his ship locked up for twenty weeks' continuance; he at length succeeded in extricating himself from his perilous situation, and returned home in the utmost disappointment, without hearing any tidings whatever of Captain Hudson, or having the least chance of finding the north-west passage.

Captain Gibbons made a similar attempt in 1614, and returned equally unsuccessful.

In the year 1615, Captain Robert Bylot, an experienced navigator, and one who was also well acquainted with the causes of mischance in former expeditions, having sailed with Hudson, Button, and Gibbons, was appointed to make another trial for a north-west passage.

Captain Bylot took with him the celebrated William Baffin to act as pilot in the arctic seas, for which duty he was peculiarly qualified on account of his experience in those icy regions, having been for many years engaged in the whale trade at Spitzbergen.

In this voyage Bylot advanced no further north than the sixty-fifth degree of latitude in Davis's Strait.

In the following year, (1616,) Bylot and Baffin proceeded to explore Davis's Strait, and succeeded in penetrating beyond the remotest advance of Davis, and the accounts say they even got up to the seventy-eighth degree, where Baffin observed the variation of the compass to be 65° W. which was then the greatest ever known. In this place those navigators came into an extensive sound, which they named Sir Thomas Smith's Sound, and which spread beyond the seventy-eighth degree. Standing over to the westward, they saw Cary's Isles, and afterwards the first sound on the American side, which Captain Bylot named Alderman Jones's Sound, and further south in lat. 74° N. Sir James Lancaster's Sound.

The observations made by Baffin in the course of this voyage impressed him strongly with the conviction that the north-west passage was still feasible; and he communicated his opinion to Mr. Briggs, the famous mathematician, who took much interest in the affair, and even made a chart* according to Baffin's information, which, with a discourse illustrative of the subject, was never made public.

The persuasion of the feasibility of a north-west passage continued to hold an influence over the public mind so strongly, that in 1631, the King, (Charles,)

* No chart has hitherto been published above the seventy-third degree of north latitude in Davis's Straits; and I indulge a presumption, that the public will receive with some gratification a chart, carefully made by myself, affording a correct view of the coast of Greenland as far as the seventy-seventh degree, including the newly-discovered Linnæan Isles.

on representation being made on the subject, gave his commands to Captain Luke Fox to proceed on the inquiry. His Majesty appeared so well satisfied of the practicability of the undertaking, that he gave Captain Fox a chart on which the passage was marked, and also a letter written by himself to be delivered to the Emperor of Japan as soon as the Captain had effected his voyage into the eastern seas. Fox, like his predecessors, roamed about in Hudson's Bay, unable to find out the expected passage, and returned home without accomplishing his mission, but still certain that a passage could be effected through some yet undiscovered opening in the northern extremity of Hudson's Bay.

Captain Fox drew his conclusions, to that effect, from the state of the tide in a distance of 250 leagues which he had traversed. "It is inconceivable," he says, "how such a vast quantity of water should be recalled and repaired every twelve hours, if it were not fed and supplied from some great and vast ocean, alluding to the northern Pacific.

Captain James, of Bristol, sailed to Hudson's Bay the same year as Captain Fox, and discovered several islands, but was nearly shipwrecked in some shallow soundings, with a rocky bottom, into which he had unexpectedly run. His researches for the north-west passage were unsuccessful.

During the same year the Danish government sent out a ship in the same pursuit, and the result was similar to those already experienced.

In 1653, the Danes, unwilling to make a second experiment in Hudson's Bay, projected a design of passing in a north-east course, through the Waygate Strait, south of Nova Zembla, and by that way to attempt a passage to India. The obstructions they experienced from the ice compelled them to abandon the undertaking, and they were forced to return as unsuccessful as former adventurers.

In the reign of Charles II. anno 1676, the Duke of York, afterwards James II., who was ever attentive to maritime concerns, at the advice of Lord Berkeley, ordered a ship to be fitted out, the command of which was given to Captain Wood, who was directed to sail in company with one of the King's ships, for the purpose of discovering a north-east passage to India. But this, like former expeditions, was frustrated by the ice, which prevented the ships from advancing beyond the seventy-sixth degree north. The misfortune of shipwreck was added to disappointment, as the King's ship came foul of a sunken rock and foundered. This accident damped the expectations of those who advocated the design, and the thing was pronounced impracticable.

The spirit of adventure, however, it appears, was not yet quite subdued, as Captain Barlow was afterwards sent out in the year 1720, by a company of private persons, to seek a passage to China through some opening in Hudson's Bay. The undertaking cost the Captain and crew their lives, the ship having been cast away in about the latitude of 63° N. when every person on board perished.

Another unsuccessful attempt was made by Capt. Scroggs in 1722. Like all the former adventurers, he failed in accomplishing his object.

In order to rectify all the supposed errors of preceding voyagers, Mr. Dobbs took the pains of collecting the amplest information on the subject, and drew up his views of the matter, in which he largely examined the nature of the currents, tides, and the other circumstances which appeared necessary to illustrate the subject.

Mr. Dobbs having communicated his information to Capt. Middleton, a gentleman, like most of his contemporaries, enthusiastically involved in the question of the north-west passage, the undertaking was again resumed.

In order the more effectually to ensure success, Capt. Middleton sailed from Churchill River, in Hudson's Bay, in the year 1741, where, by order of the Admiralty Board, he had been ordered to winter, that, by being so near to the expected place, the greatest possible advantage might accrue to the inquiry. The ships employed on this occasion were two sloops of war.

The expectations attached to this undertaking also proved fallacious, as Capt. Middleton found it impossible to proceed further north than 66° 30′ of north latitude, and returned to England greatly disappointed, and determined to oppose a project which he considered visionary and impracticable.

In consequence of the representations of Capt. Middleton on the subject, the public opinion was much divided; yet so firmly was Mr. Dobbs convinced of the truth and strength of his positions, that he hoped by perseverance to effect an object, for which, by much cherishing, he had contracted an unconquerable affection.

One opinion seemed, at this time, very much to aid the purpose of Mr. Dobbs, and to excite him to greater exertion ; and that was, that the failures of Capts. Scroggs and Middleton were in some measure effected by the endeavours of the Hudson's Bay Company, the members of which, the better to protect their monopoly in the trade of furs, took every means to stifle accounts at the factory, if such accounts appeared to throw light on the subject of the north-west passage. Such conduct was looked upon as extremely illiberal, particularly after the great expense and danger which had been incurred, and out of which the very existence of that company's monopoly originally sprang.

Mr. Dobbs, supported in his views with such a powerful argument, laboured incessantly in the affair ; and the matter appeared of such importance, that the legislature offered a reward of 20,000*l.* to such persons as would succeed in penetrating through the northern waters of the Atlantic, by a westward course, into the Pacific Ocean.

Such a bounty, as might be expected, became a most powerful stimulus to exertion, and Mr. Dobbs was gratified in seeing an expedition fitted out, in the year 1746, for the purpose of effecting his favourite project.

Accordingly, in the above year, two vessels, the Dobbs Galley, commanded by Capt. William Moore, and the California, under the command of Capt. Francis Smith, were fitted out with the utmost care for the comfort and preservation of the people. In order to afford the greater advantage to the occasion, the celebrated Mr. Henry Ellis was invited to undertake the office of agent to the company, at whose expense the outfit was made, which he cheerfully complied with, and to that gentleman the public is indebted for the best account ever before exhibited of the attempts to explore the north-west passage.

Having received very ample instructions, from which they were directed to find, according to the state of the tide, the most northerly cape of the American continent, in latitude sixty-two degrees north, the ships proceeded on their voyage, accompanied with the wishes of thousands for their success. It should be also mentioned, that the captains of those ships were cautioned against the policy of the Hudson's Bay Company. That this caution was not unnecessary was afterwards proved; for when the Dobbs and California were obliged to winter in Hudson's Bay, the governor threatened to use force to repel the intrusion. However, by the firmness and conciliatory manner of the persons intrusted with the expedition, the difficulty was got over, and the ships were comfortably, at least safely, moored for the winter at a convenient place in Hays's River.

From this place the voyagers were not able to clear, on account of the ice, till the beginning of the ensuing June. They continued throughout that summer traversing the northern extremity of Hudson's Bay, every hour in hopes of finding the long desired passage, but in vain; for after various efforts, countenanced by ingenious and plausible arguments, they were obliged to return without deriving any advantage from the voyage, except a more exact knowledge of the shores of that bay, and the manners of the natives, who met them in great numbers whenever they approached any point of the coast. One circumstance recorded on this occasion is worthy of note. Although the Esquimeaux, as they are called, are reputed savages, and are represented as mischievous and sanguinary, yet to the interference of one of those savages, the California, one of the ships, owed her preservation.

Having been thrown upon a ledge of rocks, and in danger every moment of going to pieces, the natives came around, as usual, to barter, when one old man, perceiving the danger in which the vessel lay, pointed out a deep passage, through which, when the California floated on the return of tide, they sailed in the utmost safety, the same old man paddling on before, and showing how to avoid the rocks.

Notwithstanding the failure of this last expedition in search of a north-west passage, still the arguments in favour of its practicability remained in sufficient force to impress the minds of the persons engaged in even that expedition, to expect success at some future opportunity. To this effect Mr. Ellis has left his opinion upon record, that the expected opening would be found somewhere in the north extremity of Hudson's Bay, and not in Davis's Strait; but Mr. Ellis had no knowledge of that Strait.

Since the expedition in the Dobbs and California, the subject of a passage to India northwards had been frequently discussed, but never acted on until the year 1775, when a voyage was undertaken at the request of the Royal Society, to try how far navigation was practicable towards the North Pole, and whether there existed a possibility of discovering a passage to the East Indies, by any route through those frozen regions.

The late Lord Mulgrave, then the Hon. Capt. Phipps, and Capt. (afterwards Admiral) Lutwidge, received severally the command of the Race Horse and Carcass bomb-ships, to carry this attempt into execution. All the necessary means for comfort and security were provided; nor were the concerns for scientific observation overlooked.

On the 2d of June they sailed from the Nore, being directed to steer by a particular meridian, until the presence of ice would make it necessary to alter their course to the eastward, and proceeded with very little obstruction until they reached above the eighty-first degree, where they were driven by the pressure of the ice descending from the northward, into a bay, and the ships were apparently locked up, never again to be extricated. Every exertion was made to free the ships, but in vain; for after several days' ineffectual toil in that endeavour, the commanders came to the sad resolution of abandoning them, in order to save the lives of the men. The confusion attending such a resolution is described as extreme, as each individual, anxious for his personal safety, was only concerned about his own comforts. The boats were hoisted out, with intent to drag them over the ice until they should reach the open sea.

In this dreadful alternative, of remaining to perish in that inhospitable place, or encounter the dangers of the ocean in light open boats, one of those "convulsions of nature," so frequently observed in the icy seas, relieved them from their miserable situation. The ice having accumulated against Spitzbergen, and pressed against on the western side by the unbroken field ice, in that direction, the current from the north at the same time urging the pack to the southward, the ice began to give way, and the sufferers hailed the opening with joy. They saw the ships which they had abandoned beginning to move, and immediately hastened on board, in the hope of deliverance from their perilous situation, and the wind having shifted from an easterly to a N. E. wind, which was, in fact, the cause of the "convulsion of nature," the ice gave way freely before the current, and the ships were set at liberty.

After this fortunate escape from a miserable death, the voyagers had not much spirit to persevere, nor would their endeavours, it appears, have been of much avail, as the state of the season was not favourable to the enterprise. The chart, made on the occasion, exhibits many lines of traverse made in the hope of finding the passage to the Pole; but the utmost advance effected was no further than latitude 81° 36′ N. somewhat less than Hudson had gone before.

Captain Phipps having explored thus far, and being satisfied that a passage by that way was impracticable, determined to return home, and both ships arrived in the month of October in the same year.

In this manner ended the latest attempt, having for its object the determination of a passage by the north seas to the Pacific Ocean, each undoubtedly undertaken with the most confident hope of success, in the assurance that the errors of preceding trials would enable the successor in the enterprise to avoid such, and consequently to attain a point of such desirable importance. The motives which put the adventurers into action were unquestionably fair and praiseworthy, and no impartial mind should blame their want of success. A cause wherein such men as Mr. Briggs, Mr. Dobbs, and Mr. Ellis voluntarily were engaged must, from a consideration of their talents, be of the highest respectability; but, in the present, we have not alone their valuable suffrage, but that of the whole nation, and of the legislature, that the undertaking so long and frequently attempted should not even yet be abandoned as hopeless.

Of the expedition now in contemplation, I must, in truth, pretend ignorance regarding its object and arrangement, except so far as the reports of the daily prints are designed to inform the public. From this source only, I am aware that some ships are fitted out for the purpose of exploring the long sought passage to the Indian seas by the north-west. On this subject I beg leave, as an eyewitness of the state of the globe, recently, in a high northern degree, and from a candid examination of the real state of the case, to submit a few observations on the subject, it being one in which the most important results are involved, highly beneficial if successful, and ruinous if otherwise.

CHAPTER VIII.

OF THE EXPEDITION LATELY PREPARED.

A VITAL interest of Great Britain is the extension and security of commerce. From this source, in a great measure, flow her internal grandeur, national renown, and wide dominion; and every means tending to promote commerce is consequently encouraged to the greatest degree.

After the discovery of America by Columbus, or more accurately speaking by Cabot, who was the first to touch upon the continent of North America, as we have seen in the sketch of his voyage, sanguine expectations were entertained of a possibility of finding a passage westward to the East Indies, by which the tedious voyage by the Cape of Good Hope might be avoided; and no expense was spared in fitting out ships from time to time, to have the expectation realized. New and daring adventurers came forward in hopes of winning the laurels of success, but it has been, in many instances unfortunately,—in all unsuccessfully attempted.

Mr. Dobbs calculated on finding the passage in latitude 62° N. which Mr. Ellis proved to be erroneous; and the latter with equal confidence fixed the probable opening in the north end of Hudson's Bay. Baffin, who was a practical and able navigator, well accustomed to sailing amongst ice, had acted previously on other grounds, and directed his course up Davis's Strait, and although he had not gained the point, yet he persisted in the accuracy of his plan till his death, which happened in the East Indies at the siege of Ormus.

Hudson, aware of the errors of his predecessors, tried the way both to Spitzbergen and Davis's Strait. He did not succeed in either; the ice on the eastern side presenting an eternal obstruction, and in the latter, his death prematurely cut him short before he could prove the superiority of his plans. It is to be regretted that a man so well calculated for enterprise as Hudson was, did not push forwards into Davis's Strait at once, and try to solve this great problem. In Lord Mulgrave's expedition the ideas of Hudson were again acted on; but the advance effected was not so great even as his.

This rapid review of the various expeditions is more, in point of plan, than with any regard to the succession of dates, and my reason for so doing is that, by comparing all the former in the manner in which I have done, the present design of fitting out ships for a similar enterprise may be the more easily understood.

In the former undertakings, on the subject of a north-west passage, it had been repeatedly tried on the American side, and the failure of such attempts gave an opportunity of urging an opinion that on the Spitzbergen side the design would be found more practicable. The latter opinion was found erroneous, and speculation was, from the repeated disappointments, compelled to pause.

Whilst the desolating work of war was going forward, the thought of renewing the almost forgotten affair of the passage to India, by the north-west seas, must have appeared so unfit for inquiry, that one need not wonder that since the expedition under Capt. Phipps, the subject was left for so many years unagitated. But now that "wild war's deadly blast is blown," the minds of men have been again attracted to this interesting affair; and to the honour of the Royal Society it is to be recorded, that the resuscitation of the subject is owing to their philosophical vigilance.

The great intent of the present undertaking, if I may presume to judge, seems to be, to make a grand effort at once in the sea northward of Spitzbergen, there to push forward directly to the pole, and in Davis's Strait to sail as far northward as possible, with a corresponding intent. Sailing to the north pole has been long a very favourite subject for closet lucubration; and as long as a man, in such circumstances, chooses to amuse himself harmlessly, or entertain his friends with his effusions through the medium of a magazine, such pursuits are altogether allowable; but where such visionary schemes are in contemplation as would mislead the public mind, in the same manner as the writer misleads himself, not pausing over facts, and maturely weighing their consequences, the prudent will be careful how they admit his opinions, however plausibly dressed up.

This utopian paper-built plan of sailing to the north pole has been long since defeated by the experience of navigators, who penetrated to the eighty-second degree on the Spitzbergen side of Greenland. The whale hunters have even gone to the eighty-fourth degree, and some even much higher, when the season would permit; whilst, on the other hand, many years may pass before such an opportunity will present itself, the state of the ice depending almost invariably on the state and nature of the prevailing winds, and not, as is represented to have occurred last season, on some "convulsion of nature." Again, on the Davis's Strait side of Greenland, another great difficulty occurs, arising from the same universal cause, it being found impracticable, during some years, to ascend much higher than Disko, whilst in more favourable seasons the ice clears away, and leaves the sea open for vessels to sail beyond the Frow Islands in the seventy-third degree, and sometimes to the seventy-fourth degree, or as the sailors familiarly call it, the Devil's Thumb. In some seasons, as in the last, ships can advance even further, as I have noted in my Journal account—to the seventy-eighth degree nearly, until the icy continent spreads its rocky front against further advance that way to the Pole.

Now, even were the project of sailing to the Pole a practicable one, is it inferred that in event of such a thing being done, the object of the present voyages would be accomplished? Allowing for an instant, that a ship could be brought to the extremity of latitude, until the curiosity of the contriver of such a voyage might be gratified with a sight of probably the polar star in his zenith,* to what utility could such a proceeding possibly lead? Suppose, at the same time, for the latter supposition is, at least, as likely to be cor-

* It is not possible to see the stars in high northern latitudes during the summer.

rect as the former, that there exists interminable ice,—such a mass as the icy continent which I have seen at Davis's Strait, what then, it may be asked, would be the proper and safe mode of proceeding, but to return before the season of fogs, frost, and storms should involve the incautious mariner in inevitable destruction? It is far from my disposition to treat a matter of such a serious nature with levity, nor am I fond of quotations, but I may be indulged in applying to such a design, under such circumstances as hang by the above suppositions, the words of some poet, who, describing a great military expedition, says of the commander, that he

> "Marched forty thousand up the hill,
> Then marched them down again."

For in what other light can the consequences of this polar visit be viewed but in those of absolute futility? As long as the axis of the earth remains in its present angular position, so long will ice be found in those waters, and so long will navigators find obstruction in every attempt to penetrate by the Pole towards the northern Pacific.

That the axis of the earth may have undergone some alteration, can, I presume, be very little a matter for dispute; and of this some very obvious proofs may be adduced. Among these the gradual decay of icy accumulation at the poles is the most remarkable. For many years navigators have been astonished at the frequency and magnitude of the bergs of ice islands met with in high latitudes, and numerous theories have been offered to explain their construction.

Masters in the Greenland and Davis's Strait trade, in other respects men of close observation, have to myself asserted that those immense masses must have proceeded from some great fresh-water sea near the Pole. Such persons had never seen the ice continent; but because experience had taught them to find fresh water for the supply of their ships, from pools to be found on the bergs, they of course supposed that those masses could be formed only in fresh water. In the foregoing pages, wherein ice formation is considered, the fallacy of such an opinion has been exposed; and I think this place not inappropriate to mention it again, lest any error to that effect should dwell upon the minds of such persons.

Now, by the descent of those ice bergs into lower latitudes, the great parent accumulation must be undergoing annual decay; but, as it is so rarely seen, from the vast tracts of field ice that keep it usually beyond view, little can be said with regard to its increase by annual supply. Should I be allowed to offer an opinion on the subject, I would presume to say, that the great ice continent is suffering rapid diminution, by the bursting of the bergs from its lofty sides; that nothing is added to the extent of that continent at its base, as nothing but comparatively thin field ice is there formed, and that as the bergy fragments are detached and carried to the southward, it must be evident that they must have open water for their progress in that direction.

That the passage of those bergs southward is not in uniform time, many being recognised in particular situations for years, is argument also to prove that the seas in which they move are not always open, and consequently not always accessible to shipping; and, with regard to this, the variableness of the winters in the north should be taken into account, some being dreadfully severe, whilst others are mild and fit to be endured by the human constitution. Thus the native inhabitants of Greenland are capable of enduring much severity of cold, but in very inclement winters they are comparatively as sensible of extraordinary cold as Europeans. Even the birds of passage and other migratory animals exhibit similar sensations. But here it is worthy of mention, that when the winter in southern latitudes is known to be severe, the subsequent or preceding winter in Greenland is mild, and it is then not unusual to see birds migrating to the northward from southern latitudes to enjoy the milder climate of Greenland.

This evidence of severity of climate does not therefore depend on the presence of ice; it must be sought for in a far different cause: not but that where ice is present a greater degree of cold is experienced; but, from my own experience, I declare that the most intolerable heat I ever suffered was felt at a moment when I was standing up to the knees in snow on a wide field of ice in 70° of N. latitude, and such a recollection is impressed upon my mind from that circumstance, that I should not like to make the experiment a second time. The Uskee children sit and play upon the snow with their heads uncovered in the same manner as European children enjoy the pleasures of the grassy green; and the adult Uskee sleeps with tranquillity and comfort on the snow: so do likewise such Danes or other foreigners as accustom themselves from choice or necessity to the habits of the natives.

In a design to penetrate the arctic regions, either by the eastern or western side of Greenland, primary attention must be given to the nature of the ice to be met with in those very different waters. The accounts of persons who annually visit the seas around Spitzbergen, agree in representing that island as utterly uninhabitable in the winter months, and by reason of this apprehension the attempt has never yet been made. If any such ever yet occurred, the event is unknown to me; but the consequences of such an attempt, even arising from necessity in case of shipwreck, may be easily presumed on natural grounds. The land, like that of Old Greenland, is mostly bare rock, in some scanty spots under the influence of the sun, in summer showing forth its cryptogamic tenants, as if the beauties of expended fructification could not be displayed in such a desert soil. Man is capable of enduring much; but a climate in 80° could not be sufficiently genial to prolong life in a place which every animal is known to desert on the approach of winter, and all nature is clad in the shroud of death, and mourned over by the howling storm.

The shore of Greenland, west in its most northern extremity as it presents itself in 74° N. is inhabited, but whether throughout the winter is rather a doubtful circumstance. The natives of that country are guided by a simple but prudent policy, which affords little information to strangers, regarding their economy, but what can be gleaned by observation. In summer they have been seen so high as that latitude; but from the view I have had of the Linnæan Isles, even in the late universally open season, I am inclined to think that they do not dwell so far to the northward as those islands are situate. I rather think they remove to the southward in winter.

The extreme dangers to be encountered in those high latitudes, when once the indications of winter's setting in appear, are incalculable. Though the field ice be at that period broken up, accumulated in packs, dispersed, or even dissolved, still by those several changes the cold, increasing in proportion as the sun moves (apparently) to the southward, condenses the vapour with which the atmosphere is loaded, and foggy weather succeeds, often rather suddenly, and in such density and extent, as to make the situation of a ship doubtful to the mariner, and if in the neighbourhood of bergs the vessel is in danger of momentary destruction.

This part of the subject, I am aware, is prematurely introduced, but in the reader's indulgence I request it may be allowed to remain, and that the observation be kept in recollection: we shall see its utility and wholesome application shortly.

In hinting the probability of a change in the axis of the earth having taken place, I did not intend that I should be understood to say that such a change was sudden, but imperceptibly gradual. It is not for my humble pen to intrude on the province of the astronomer; but a thought has suggested itself to my mind, that the matter may be determined simply by measuring the circle which the earth's axis forms in revolution round the polar star, when, if found not exactly the same as heretofore, the influence will obviously and fairly be, that some change has taken place. If such a change has occurred, it will justly be considered a matter worthy of discussion among persons conversant in such subjects, to determine whether the centrifugal action may not aid in demolishing that icy hoard in the north of Greenland, which, I apprehend, encompasses the north pole. I feel that this suggestion places me on ticklish ground; I therefore beg permission to transfer the subject to abler hands.

Independently however of the influence of the sun on the ice continent, or on its huge bergy fragments during the summer months, or even were the proofs of the suggestion right regarding the probable effects of the centrifugal force, another cause exists to retard or promote the formation of ice, (I mean the flat or ordinary field ice,) and subsequently contribute to its destruction. The cause to which I allude is the operation of the wind, which, in all its changes, reigns the tyrant of the arctic world. To explain this it will be necessary to examine the matter in a very few points only.

The reader has seen in the course of my Journal, from the time of entering Davis's Strait and meeting with the ice, a faithful record of every wind that blew, and its effects on the atmosphere, as indicated by the thermometer. That part of the Journal is devested of every comment, in order that those effects should meet the eye, and satisfy the mind at once. The plan has been continued up to Disko in the seventieth degree, and resumed with the progress of the Journal to the Linnæan Isles, and down again to the seventy-fourth degree, when the indications of approaching winter commenced.

I shall now copy an extract from a Journal kept by Crantz, during a winter in Greenland. I shall abridge it so as not to tire the reader with details.

September.—Wind N. E. warm; wind S. very warm; wind S. storm.

October.—Wind N. E. snow; wind N. E. storm and cold; wind S. storm and snow.

November.—Wind N. E. excessively cold; wind S. E. storm and snow dust; wind S. storm.

December.—Lightning; afterwards S. E. winds.

January.—Wind N. and N. E. cold in earnest; more mild in the end.

February.—Wind N. and N. E. extreme cold; then rain: thawing E. and S. winds; cold and rain.

From the foregoing extract it may be observed, that the cold of winter sets in early in September, (the months being dated on the first day of each,) and that the prevailing winds throughout the months of that season are E. N. or N. E., and these are connected with the expressions, cold, snow, storm and cold, excessively cold, storm and snow dust, excessively cold, and cold in earnest. The latter phrase the reader must interpret for himself.

Mr. Ellis, who, as has been mentioned, remained during a winter in Hudson's Bay, states that the winter began there in the latter end of September, with sleet and large flakes of snow. When the wind was westerly or southerly, the cold was very supportable; but when the wind was northerly, or north-westerly, it was excessively keen, with drift snow as small as grains of sand.

From a glance back to my Journal, it will be seen that in the summer months, northerly, north-easterly, or easterly winds, promote the process of freezing. The extract from Crantz's Journal shows that those winds prevail in winter, at which time the field ice is formed in the arctic seas; and Ellis's account of northerly winds exercising dominion and similar influence in Hudson's Bay, aids the conclusion that those winds, continuing to blow during the winter, must produce that great field of ice which extends across the frozen seas properly so denominated.

On the contrary, by referring to the observations of both the above-mentioned writers, it will be found that westerly or southerly winds produce an increased temperature in the air, which leads to a solution of the ice in the early summer months, more especially in Davis's Strait; and the record in my Journal is additional evidence of this fact. So that on those extremities of the icy plain, the first open spaces must evidently occur on the south-western side.

Now, the influence of the sun, as the summer advances, taking effect upon the ice, disposes it to split; and the first wind that agitates the surface of the sea, causes a swell, by means of which the whole is broken up. Subsequently, the solution of the ice helps to swell the current, and it only requires the action of a northerly or easterly wind, to drive the broken ice into packs, which are afterwards carried down to the southward or westward, and there finally dissolved.

The importance of considering the state of the winds in the northern seas, and their effects, both in the winter and summer seasons, appeared very great, for the following reasons:

In the first place, no vessel can navigate those seas in winter on account of the excessive cold; the surface of the sea being covered over with ice. Secondly, because the ice does not begin to break up till the month of April, and sometimes till the latter end of May, when the wind blows from S. and W. And lastly, because it is impossible for any ship or other vessel to proceed into high latitudes, unless an easterly, northerly, or north-easterly wind has previously occurred, to clear away the ice, and render the passage northward free.

Having now examined the points most material to be reflected on, regarding the navigation of the frozen seas, it appears a convenient and proper place to offer a few remarks on the precise subject of the north-west passage through those seas, into the North Pacific Ocean, and thence to Japan, China, the East Indies, and also to the west coasts of America.

The brief sketch of the numerous attempts made in former years to explore the north-west passage, which has been submitted to the reader in the preceding pages, would appear quite sufficient to warrant the conclusion that all hopes of its practicability, by the way of Hudson's Bay, vanished with the failure of the expedition recorded by Ellis in the voyage of the Dobbs and California. And yet, though that disappointment evidently weighed heavy on the minds of the adventurers in that expedition, still so strong was the infatuation attending the project, that the historian of that failure takes leave of his subject with recommending further trials in Chesterfield's Inlet or Repulse Bay.

The discredit thrown on the plan by the attempts to penetrate to India by a north-east passage, will not be brought forward as an inducement to make any further exertions in that direction; and I have little doubt on my mind, that the design of sailing to the North Pole, in the intent of making that a way to India, if now put in execution, will not be repeated soon.

CHAPTER VIII.

OF THE ONLY ROUTE BY WHICH SUCCESS MAY BE ATTAINED.

There remains only one other direction as yet unexplored, in which to make further attempts for this great desideratum in navigation; and that is, in Davis's Strait, in a high latitude.

Bylot and Baffin penetrated very far to the northward—as report says, to the seventy-eighth degree of north latitude. Those navigators, it seems, were desirous of proceeding to the North Pole also; however that may be, they changed their minds, and, proceeding westward, discovered the land on the American side, where they gave name to a sound; and, without affording any better lights to guide conjecture by, without exploring that sound or the one to the north-westward of it, they forthwith went to the southward, equally unmindful of any opening along the coast, yet occasionally coming in sight of land, and so returned home.

Now Mr. Ellis and others, who examined the bottom of Hudson's Bay, observed the current always coming from the northward, precisely in the direction of the sound named by Baffin, and more particularly of the great sound beyond that. Such a current could easily find its way through even very broken lands and narrow channels, and have an abundant supply from the solution of the arctic ice.

Here then is a rational and ample field for an accurate investigation; and if those persons who are engaged to explore the north-west passage need a stronger impulse than the honour of deciding this long agitated question, or the more solid splendour of a share in the golden reward, I shall ask their permission to put them in possession of a fact of some consequence to the attainment of success.

Some of the whale ships which had proceeded furthest north in the course of last summer in Davis's Strait, as may be seen in my Journal, got embarrassed amongst packed ice, and, as they were so circumstanced, were in extreme danger. It was necessary to wait for the aid of some friendly wind to extricate them, which, very fortunately, soon came to their relief. Whilst in that situation, the master of one, being, as usual, stationed in the hurricane-house, near the mast head, on looking westward and northward, observed the sea become clear to an interminable extent in that direction, and the surface soon after began to swell and rise, which are the surest indications of an extensive sea, and these motions shortly cleared away the pack, when no obstruction appeared to prevent him sailing as far to the north-west as inclination might urge; but the season being then so far advanced, that to remain any longer would be dangerous beyond calculation, and his oath being in the way of research, as well as the whales having disappeared,—all these considerations were sufficient to compel his immediate return. On this fact I shall make no comment further than putting a short query.

Had the commander of a ship been so circumstanced as to have a door of such an inviting description thrown open before him to the north-west, and that in the seventy-sixth degree of north latitude, in the middle of July, when the fogs were about to set in, would he think it adviseable to proceed to the north-west, and take chance of the casualties of ice driven thither before him, and probably covering the coast, which by embarrassing his progress might compel him to remain longer than he otherwise would wish?

I may take the liberty of stating, moreover, that in consequence of the ice descending from the northward in the beginning of the season, and driving chiefly to the south-west, any attempt at penetrating to the north-west by that course is considered quite impracticable and extremely dangerous; so that the east coast of James's Island is never seen by navigators going out, and in latter years seldom by those returning homewards.

The opportunities, then, which I have had of observing the actual state of the arctic seas, have produced on my mind a conviction that it is practicable for ships to find a passage from the Atlantic into the Pacific Ocean, by the shores of North America, and that that passage is to be effected above the seventy-fourth degree of north latitude. The various appearances of the ice found in those seas, and the effects produced from congelation, are of eminent importance in the consideration of the present subject, as all the discoveries hitherto made in the frozen regions have terminated with the ice.

In Cooke's voyages it appears, that the state of the ice forbade an approach to the North Pole much above Behring's Strait. To this point, I wish to apply a few observations. Open sea is always favourable to the solution of ice, from the great agitation of the surface, ice being invariably formed in a state of rest. In support of this the reader is requested to refer to a fact stated in that part of the observations which regarded ice formation :—whenever the ship came within an extent of recent congelation a calm ensued. That such could not be accidental, was evident from its invariable recurrence in similar circumstances, and that too when the presence of land was so remote as not to aid in producing any change of wind. It certainly appeared to me an unusual occurrence, that a vessel under full but easy way, should be at once arrested in her progress by causes not obvious to common view ; yet such was the case whenever the ship's course lay through an extent of nascent ice.

It has been also observed, that the water surface in the vicinity of field-ice is usually tranquil, and therefore dangerous to ships in case of a strong wind pressing on the distant extremity of the field, or any other cause, such as currents, projecting rocks, or heavy bergs urging forward the mass. In such a case, it must be obvious the danger chiefly arises from the apparent security, as the inexperienced would consider the tranquillity of his station to be indicative of the absence of danger ; but should the ice begin to move, a vessel so circumstanced must drift before it, and have to encounter the hidden dangers of the deep, or, in the event of a gale, to meet the awful consequences of the ice becoming packed, when, if surrounded by those heavy fragments, there is scarcely a chance of escape. The sailors accustomed to those situations are very expert in determining the course of the packed ice, and measure with singular accuracy the physical pressure of each piece likely to come in contact with the ship. Where an open space in the pack appears sufficiently large to admit of manœuvring the vessel, it is usually entered, until some opening is observable. Such an open space is called a hole of water, in the language of the whale hunters.

In the works of writers who have described the Alps, mention is made of extensive beds of ice occupying the higher valleys among those mountains. Those are denominated glaciers, which appears to be an appropriate term. Though remote from the subject in question, with regard to distance, the introduction of the Alpine glaciers in this place may be allowed, and the brevity of my observation will help to excuse the introduction. The Alps, on account of their great elevation, are mostly covered with snow, which in the summer months is dissolved, and carried down to the valleys. The valleys are met with in different elevations, for which reason the temperature of those places is at all times different. The dissolved snow, under such different degrees of temperature, must be, in the more elevated valleys, converted into ice, which, in turn, is again reduced to a fluid state as the atmosphere becomes more heated ; and hence the origin of those many streams, torrents, lakes and navigable rivers which derive their tribute from Alpine sources. It is not, however, always the case that the dissolved ice and snow can reach the lower situations without diminution. Many of those valleys are confined pits, the solid surrounding rocks affording no outlet for the accumulated waters, which being so confined, and in a great elevation, invariably become ice, which is rarely afterwards dissolved. Each succeeding year increases its volume, and the glacier is formed. Such is the progress of glacier ice in Switzerland. There it is known to lie only in elevated situations; but not having at hand a scale of such elevations, I must request the reader to make that very needful reference.

In the southern parts of Greenland, the elevations are much more considerable than the more northern. In those parts therefore glacier ice may have been seen; such probably as has shut up the western extremity of Frobisher's Strait, and rendered that way no longer passable to navigators. Indeed there is one very remarkable place on the western coast of Greenland, which the Danes call the Eis Blink, and which I have every reason to think is nothing more than a monstrous berg, which by some "revolution of nature," such as a contrary wind, and the great indraught which is known to exist on those shores, had many years since been forced into that situation.

In Greenland further north, from Reef Koll to the great basaltic Disko, the land becomes remarkably low and rounded, few mountains there appearing. The existence therefore of glacier ice cannot be, in those places, probable. The intersections of Greenland by its numerous internal waters are, however, difficult of investigation from the fiords,* sounds, and other entrances being blocked up by the bergy ice, which obstructs the passage of such field, or packed ice, as descends from the internal waters; for it may be received as an axiom, that, in extensive seas, there is the readiest solution of ice.

From Disko to the northward the land gradually becomes less elevated, an odd eminence occasionally appearing above the descending line, until the most remote lands are buried in the polar ice, which beyond the Linnæan Isles is seen to out-top the rocky prominences.

From what cause the accumulation of polar ice has arisen is extremely difficult, if not impossible, to determine. The depression of the earth's axis, during the great change which gave the globe its present appearance, might be assumed as a prevailing cause. The presence of the sun, were there no declination, would extend a steady degree of temperature towards both poles, and would in that case forbid the great accumulation of ice, which, during the months of winter, is at present known to occur.

To the same cause, if the supposition be admitted,

* Fiord, pronounced feuor, is the space between two projecting mountains, the bottom being narrower as the bases of the promontories descend in the sea, into which they dip sometimes steeply, but generally otherwise, as has been determined by soundings, which are always more shallow near the rocks than more remotely; so that the jutting base of the rock on both sides may be distinctly traced by sounding towards the middle of the fiord. There is generally shoal water or a rocky reef in the neighbourhood of a fiord, which may be easily distinguished from the other inlets by the land being visible at its inner extremity, and from a bay by its very narrow appearance. It is therefore adviseable to keep a good offing when near any of those fiords.

the destruction of the polar icy continent or glacier may be assigned—the operation of the sun's rays, and also the centrifugal action of the earth aiding that operation. Under this double influence, the immense bergs are rent off from the original mass, borne southwards by the prevailing current, and occasionally urged by the wind, and seldom pass the latitude of Staten Hook before they become finally dissolved. Now if this destruction go on for some years longer, the icy continent must at length disappear; such immense fragments being annually torn from its sides, and no increase supplying their place, those seas will become open at an earlier period than heretofore, and consequently more generally and safely navigable. In that event, which is predicted in the genuine spirit of a conviction of its accuracy, and I would add certainty, it may not be irrelevant to add some observations regarding Disko Island, as it may hereafter stand connected with the concerns of British commerce.

CHAPTER IX.

OF THE IMPORTANCE OF DISKO IN THE CASE OF SUCCESS.

THE island of Disko is of great elevation, as I have said, being more than 6000 feet perpendicular above the sea level, on its southern side, which at Fortune Bay lies in the latitude of 69° 10′ N. but runs into a low point at its northern extremity, in the Mallegat Sound, which is about the latitude 70° 18′ N. measuring in its greatest length more than one nautical degree. The general form of the island is triangular. The great body of the land of Disko is formed of basaltic columns of irregular pile, but sufficiently marked to decide their character. The southern, interior and western parts, particularly the latter, are lofty table land, with fine deep harbours, which are safe retreats for shipping when the ice begins to break up and descend to the southward, except when southerly or westerly winds happen to blow; but against any danger in those cases a very little care would afford ample security. On the southern extremity, from Fortune Bay to Lievely, there are fine situations for harbours; but being at present in a state of nature, they present little to attract the notice of a cursory visiter. Towards the eastward, the land declines from the westward and northward until at Flat-foot Shore it imperceptibly becomes strand. On the north-eastern side, the shore is skirted with very lofty peaks, some of which are said to stretch their shadow across the Waygat Sound, which is in one place twenty-five miles over. Of that circumstance, however, I am not certain; but one of those peaks is visible above the greater part of the western side of Disko.

To the southward of Disko lies South-east Bay; within which are seen some groups of low islands. Among these the western islands are situate at the south-western extremity, and are inhabited very numerously by Uskees. The whole islands are also much inhabited by the same people; and, at the latter place, the Danish officer who superintends the colony is usually resident, but occasionally removes to Lievely. The Dog Islands, Green Islands, and all the other islands sprinkled along the coast around South-east Bay, are peopled with Uskees, and are their favourite residence.

It is not usual to find South-east Bay covered with the ice after the end of June; but it frequently is closed until about the beginning or middle of that month. In the latter part of the summer, after the whalers have departed, it is usually quite clear of ice, and, in the months of August and September, the numbers of whales that resort to this bay, on their return to the southward, are represented to be incredible. The Waygat Sound, in the latter season, is also frequently open, and more certainly after an easterly or north-easterly wind has been for some time blowing, and is, in such case, a safe and commodious way for vessels to proceed northward. The Mallegat Sound, between Hare Island and Disko, is not safe, on account of the dangerous rocks which lie numerously near the land on both sides. North-east Bay, and Jacob's Bay, or Bight, as it is sometimes called, are principal retreats for the whale, which in some years is killed there in great number. Bergy Bay, to the northward of Jacob's Bay, is dangerous on account of the great number of ice bergs, which are carried in thither by a strong current running constantly round the point called Black Hook, and are there shoaled, and remain in their positions for years. Black Hook is a low bluff head, with table summit, from which circumstance it is easily distinguished. For the remaining parts of the coast northward, I beg leave to refer to the second part of my Journal.

From South-east Bay, many passages to the interior waters of Greenland are known to exist; but from many causes, they remain unexplored. To the supineness of the few Danes residing in those places that neglect is to be attributed. On being sent into those parts they sink into an habitual languor, more remarkable than even the characteristic tranquillity of the natives. Such habits unfit the Danes for much exertion, and they consequently drag out the years of their banishment in a state of inactivity; whilst even such of that nation as, from their superior station, have an interest in remaining, scarcely do more than collect the scanty superfluities of the natives, for which some trifling articles are given in exchange. The natives moreover, intent only on their seal hunting and other aquatic pursuits, if successful, are totally regardless of the future, and give themselves no concern about nautical discoveries. To the whale hunters, as at present bound by law, accident only can afford an opportunity of knowing any thing of the matter. From one of the latter I succeeded in extorting by some address the following communication, which he said he had received from an old master in the Davis's Strait trade.

"In Makkelik Ouit there is an entrance to a great inland sea. So also there is a leading from Jacob's Bight, probably into the same, through which two frigates, supposed to be English, endeavoured to penetrate; but one had been involved in such difficulties that she never returned, and was lost with all on board. The name of one was the Active, Actinix, or Actæon. In North-east Bay a passage of the same kind is also known for more than forty miles inwards. In the latter passage the islands were observed to lie in some places not more than a mile distant from each other, but lying more remotely further inwards, when, at the distance above mentioned, the view was open sea as far as the eye could reach."

If the above information be correct, which I have little reason to doubt, from the singular value set upon the communication by the person who made it, as well as the great unwillingness evinced on the occasion, it may hereafter serve some important purpose, for which end I have inserted the matter nearly in the terms in which I received it.

The expectations attached to the expedition at present preparing to go into Davis's Strait, lead me to hope that the information which I have given in the foregoing pages, regarding the ice met with in those waters, will be found useful to those who proceed with that expedition. I am not less anxious, however, to be heard attentively on the present point, namely, the importance of Disko, as connected with the events arising from the expedition.

I would at once propose that the British government should get possession of the island of Disko, and all the lands adjacent to south-east. The present wretched state of that colony renders it of little value to Denmark; but in the hands of Great Britain it would be rendered of great importance in many points of view. On account of the insignificant appearance of the place, as it now stands, government would find it not difficult to obtain possession of it; and in the course of one summer it might be placed in such a state of respectability and comfort, as would enable an English colony to attach itself to such a residence; and in the event of the strait becoming more frequented, in consequence of the discovery of the north-west passage, it is indispensably requisite that a proper force should be established, either at Lievely, or some of the islands in South-east Bay, to be at hand for the protection of British commerce, in case of any future misunderstanding with other states. When the advantages of such a design come to be known sufficiently, this plan will appear the more necessary.

The situation of Lievely is peculiarly adapted for the establishment of such a colony, as it possesses a snug harbour, naturally protected by islands on the west side, and the high rock of Disko, called the Black Land, which overhangs the sea to the eastward of the harbour, and defends it from the ice. The skirt of Disko on the south side is low, in comparison with the general elevation of the mountain, which rises almost in a perpendicular front, and at an average distance of two miles from the sea to where the rock rises most abruptly. The approach to the bold rock from the shore is extremely irregular, and shelving in extensive beds, bearing a rude resemblance to roads unskilfully hewn from the rocky ascent. This low broken skirt extends nearly from the Black Land to Fortune Bay, and consists entirely of bare rock, in many places covered with lichens of beautiful colours, and interspersed with a timid willow, (salix reticulata,) which creeps along the face of the rock, unable to rise before the bleak and withering winds. Numerous alpine plants are exposed when the sun has dissolved the snow, but these experience but a transient existence, and can be collected only during a short period in summer.

At that season the sun exerts surprising force along this space, in which Lievely is of course included. The accumulation of heat is then so great that all vegetable life is rapidly evolved, and the situation of Lievely becomes pleasant. The whale ships having already arrived, or proceeded to the northward, increase the comfort of the natives by the coarse articles which they give them in exchange for their sealskin dresses, and all becomes bustle, activity, and enjoyment. It is then also the Greenlander experiences that happiness which attaches him to his dreary home, which he would not exchange for such useless luxuries as warmer climates could afford. Such he wants not, nor covets, unless in the pernicious consequence of having been enticed to know them. A curious circumstance attends even a temporary residence in those regions. Any person who has once visited those places feels an unaccountable desire to see them again, until frequent visits render it almost habitual. For this reason, I am inclined to think that, were a British colony settled there, enjoying the superior comforts which they could command every year by the return of the whalers, in a few years the people would be not only reconciled to their situation, but even attached to the place.

If well provided, and properly trained for the purpose, the colonists might, in the latter season, kill so many whales as would enable them to amass large fortunes, when, if they chose, and the necessary regulations would permit, they might return to spend the rest of their life in affluence and ease. This is by no means an idle speculation, as I am certain many of the persons now engaged in the whale trade would be found ready to embrace such a proposal, and furnish active and skilful hands to take advantage of the after season, if secure and comfortable accommodations during winter were provided.

Ships going out in the spring could convey the necessary materials of wood and other articles for building, by way of ballast, and carry also such clothing and provisions as would be wanted at the colony, taking back the produce of the whale in return. Or were Newfoundland made an entrepot between the colony and home, more than one voyage every summer might be effected between Disko and Newfoundland, which, affording greater facilities, would add much to the importance of the new colony. Here however I deem it adviseable to guard against the mischiefs of monopoly, not to suffer a few interested individuals to take advantage of that station, as such a proceeding would defeat the valuable consequences arising from the passage by the north west, or rather by the arctic shores of North America. Government, by holding the place in possession for the common benefit of all, will thereby make it a national concern, and the public at large will benefit by the measure.

The stone materials for building are so easily raised, as they lie loosely on each other in basaltic form, that in the course of an incredibly short time a respectable fortress might be erected in any point the most eligible, at, or near Lievely, as may be determined by a competent engineer. Those materials will not require much labour to bring them into shape, and may in the first instance be placed in their natural form, and the building can afterwards be beautified in proportion as the advantages of the colony may be known. By that means a mole may be easily extended across the islands at Lievely, which will serve both as a military defence, and a shelter for vessels which may happen to remain there for the winter. A similar work will protect that little harbour on the eastward; it will then afford anchorage for fifty ships, and be a secure retreat in every season when the ice is broken up.

The situation of Lievely is commanded only from the lofty summit of Disko, which, from its great elevation, is nearly inaccessible, and can be approached only from the south-eastern extremity at Flat-foot shore; and to this latter place an enemy could not venture to approach without being seen from Lievely, and counteracted in his plans. A single observation will decide that point. During the summer months there is no night at Disko, as every person in the least acquainted with the globe must know. During that period therefore the regular succession of guard could not fail to detect the presence of any hostile force, and precautions could be easily taken to render any attempt unavailing.

Disko, therefore, becomes important in consideration of its capabilities of affording a comfortable residence during the winter, at which time the N.W., N., and N.E. winds prevail, against the severity of which a colony fixed at Lievely would be completely sheltered; and if well housed with plenty of fuel, coal being found in the lands to the eastward of South-east Bay, the business of casking the whale fat (blubber) might well be carried on during the winter, and the ships made ready for sea at the first opening of the ice. Besides, as a convenient depot for goods conveyed by ships sailing by the new passage, and carrying on an intercourse with the Pacific Ocean, the importance of Disko becomes incalculably great.

When viewed in this regard, and its facilities duly considered, it will be evident that the earliest opportunity should be taken to secure the possession of a place of such importance to the British interests. In fact a due regard for the concerns of expected commerce with the Indian nations by the northern route, will demand the possession of that particular station for the proper protection of that commerce, as it may be confidently asserted that both the American, and the Russian commerce will be pushed into the Indian seas by the same course, and a rivalry of trade will be among the consequences. The dignity of the crown and of the nation is moreover deeply concerned, not to suffer the national honour to be compromised or insulted, to both which evils that honour is exposed, unless such a station as Disko is secured; for no other place in Davis's Strait so well suits that object.

The Danish government, crippled by the late naval war, was unable to extend her protection, even if so inclined, to her Greenland subjects. This was evident in a proceeding which was little creditable to the assailants. The master of one of the whale ships, in the course of the war, not having had success in his voyage, landed at one of those miserable settlements, and plundered the people of whatever oil, blubber, whalebone, or skins, they possessed, and carried the spoil on board his ship in triumph. No opposition could be made; the poor people therefore submitted, being informed that England and Denmark were at war. No inquiry was ever instituted on the subject, and restitution, I believe, never made to the persons so plundered. A schooner and a small sloop are the only Danish vessels usually seen at Lievely, and they are kept for the purpose of collecting the produce of the miserable trade at present existing there. It may therefore be insisted that little difficulty can lie in the way of obtaining the transfer of Disko from the Danes, as it appears to them rather a burden than a benefit, and a trifling equivalent must be sufficient to satisfy their claim regarding it. The unwillingness of that government to maintain a connexion with Greenland has appeared invariably in every period of its history; and the placing of the poor Uskees under the advantages of the English constitution will be to them the greatest blessing. This I mention with the greater confidence from the partiality which they even now evince towards the crews of British ships, and their hesitating not to express their dislike of the Danes.

The natives of Greenland will have a strong inducement to accept of such a change, as the importation of English cloth amongst them will help to increase their comforts. The coarsest kind will be acceptable to them, and their industry will be encouraged to provide for the market the seal-skin dresses, which, prepared in the Uskee manner, are indispensable to the sailors frequenting Davis's Strait. The Uskee jackets (called watry pook, probably an imitation of the word water proof) are impermeable to water; so also are the trowsers, gloves, and boots, which are all made of the skins of seals deprived of the hair. The form in which the jackets are cut is very neat, and the whole dress looks well when decorated with seals' teeth, which is usually done in a very tasteful manner. When the sailor apprehends wet or severe weather he is generally dressed in the Uskee fashion, and is then regardless of the storm, having all his under dress dry and comfortable. There are numerous other advantages accruing to the native Greenlanders from such a change; but to those it may be considered superfluous to draw the reader's attention.

To the design of taking possession of Disko, it may be objected, that the distance at which it lies from any British port, and its being for so many months locked up by ice, would render the expense of retaining a barren spot like it unprofitable. To this a satisfactory reply is ready. The animals which abound in the seas all around Disko, will, by their capture, repay much more than the expense even of establishing a colony there, were no ulterior object in view; and a little labour will be sufficient to make it, as a military post, impregnable. As to the objection about its being so long locked up by ice, the same might also be urged against the Baltic and Archangel trade. Such objections are, therefore, weak and unavailing to such as seriously consider the importance of the subject. The comfort of the colony in winter can be rendered as complete in Disko as it is in many northern parts of the Russian empire, where the use of stoves counteracts the effects of cold as great, I am confident, as will be ever experienced at Disko. The late inventions of the uses of steam in heating apartments may be applied to the same purpose in Disko as elsewhere; so that a Greenland habitation may hereafter be found comfortable even to a luxurious degree.

In the event of the north-west passage being determined, vessels aided by easterly and northerly winds in the beginning of the season may run across westward, probably before the heavy ice comes down, and in their return eastward, the westerly and northerly winds, which prevail much on the American side in the latter season, together with the current, which is always in a southerly direction, will enable them to effect their passage across the arctic sea. In both those instances Disko will present a favourable resting place, either to remain at during winter, or to leave such goods as may be thought necessary for the colony, or for the purpose of procuring a supply of water, which is constantly flowing from the summits of Disko through some of the numerous channels in its rocky sides. A further reason may be adduced why that situation for a colony is very adviseable, nay, most necessary: accidents may occur in the arctic seas, from which serious consequences may arise to vessels engaged either in the whale fisheries, as they are called, or in the Pacific Ocean trade; and in such circumstances the ports of Disko, presenting a favourable retreat, can be said to offer an encouragement to the distressed mariner to make every endeavour in overcoming his difficulties in order to reach such a secure asylum. The dangers of those seas would thereby become diminished, as the increasing information, derivable from the numerous and varied courses of shipping, would ascertain the real, and remove the imaginary dangers of the voyage.

Such beneficial consequences would not be confined to Davis's Strait alone, much less to the shores of Disko. The experience of each succeeding year, by adding to the stock of nautical and philosophical science, would enable the navigator and the closeted philosopher to unite in effecting a junction between experience and abstract reasoning, mutually beneficial to the cause of commerce and of general science, and productive of a third good effect—the advancement of the great cause of humanity.

I shall proceed to examine, in as concise a compass as possible, the probable results of the expedition. In this respect I have to hope that the vanity of prophecy may not be ascribed as my motive. Having seen much of the arctic seas, all the varieties of ice formation, as well as under what peculiar causes its destruction is every year effected, and having pointed out to observation the destination of such portions as are not usually dissolved in the early parts of the season, it may be allowable to indulge a little effort of imagination in tracing out a line across the arctic ocean, in which the famed passage is most likely to be effected.

CHAPTER X.

CONCLUDING OBSERVATIONS ON A NORTH-WEST PASSAGE.

THE various attempts hitherto made for the discovery of the north-west passage to the Indian seas are already before the reader. The causes of disappointment in these attempts have been likewise detailed. One only point appears to remain unexplored, which, unfortunately for the meritorious Baffin, was not examined in his last expedition. It is not fair to attribute that failure to Baffin, or even Bylot. Any one little conversant with the perpetual annoyance of obstacles occurring in icy seas, and such as early navigators in those regions have to experience, cannot be supposed well able to determine on the conduct of such men as Baffin and Bylot when involved among ice, and remote from lands with which they were familiar, and in quest of others "which they knew not of." The greatest praise is due to such men for their intrepidity, and to them particularly who made such a mighty attempt even before the legislature had decreed the sum of money which has been since held forth as an inducement to the completion of the discovery.

It must have been somewhere near Devil's Thumb that the route of Baffin was continued, as related, to the seventy-eighth degree ; but as the land along that quarter is low and declining rapidly in descent as it approaches the Pole, and also verges much to the eastward, such a course could not be productive of beneficial consequences to inquiry after the north-west passage. Such a way was likely to be as unsuccessful as the design of sailing to the North Pole. The relation of the return of those navigators is equally mysterious. Whether, in their return from lands in the seventy-eighth degree, they had succeeded in sailing to the northward of the chain of the Linnæan Isles, and consequently to the northward of the great accumulation of ice beyond them, is not known. That they saw on their return some islands, which are called Cary's Islands, and sounds (of course lands) on the western side of Davis's Strait, or Baffin's Bay, is a circumstance which is also involved in obscurity. With that however the present question has no immediate concern; but I cannot let the term Baffin's Bay pass without remark. Any water, to constitute a bay, must be embraced by land: such, for instance, as is Hudson's Bay; but if there appear no land to the northward of Baffin's Bay, as I presume is the fact, then future geographers will designate that portion of the globe differently from what has been heretofore done. The present expedition, if properly furnished with men of scientific qualification, as I have no doubt it will be under the direction of the Royal Society, will return with store of materials to furnish the most accurate and ample information on this subject.

Mr. Ellis, in his voyage with the Dobbs and California, found the current always setting from the northward, even in places where no opening in that direction was perceivable. It is true, he also observed the tide running successively the contrary way; but still his mind was impressed with the firmest conviction that a sailing passage must be found in a northern direction in the bottom of Hudson's Bay. He even pointed out the choice of two places where the passage was to be effected; and that, from his view of the great supply of water always coming from the northward. It does not appear that any attempt has been since made on Mr. Ellis's suggestion; and as no refutation of his opinion can be advanced, his suggestion remains in undiminished credit.

Mr. Hearn, in traversing a portion of the North American continent, came in view of the sea, which then appeared extending interminably to the northward, and free from ice. This was probably some great bay belonging to the Arctic Ocean, and which will most likely be traversed by the ships of the expedition. That this expectation is not unsupported by facts will not be denied.

In the first place, the voyagers in Hudson's Bay found a northern current setting into that bay to the southward. Ice bergs have been also seen in Hudson's Bay; but, as Mr. Ellis relates, rarely to the northward; his directions being to keep as much to the northward as possible, those parts being usually free from ice. Now we have seen that ice exists only in tranquil water, and, of course, where a strong current, or much agitation of the sea, is observable, the dissolution of ice is a certain consequence. If therefore Mr. Ellis found the ice less frequent in the northern parts of Hudson's Bay, where a strong current was known to run, it naturally follows that the current descended from the Arctic Ocean, dissolving the ice in its progress, or leaving the congealed masses behind among the rocky channels leading from that water into Hudson's Bay.

Either of those deductions is unfavourable therefore to the prosecution of a passage to the Pacific by the bottom of Hudson's Bay; the former by presenting the difficulties arising from an impetuous current, and the apprehended obstructions of masses of ice and shelving rocks; the latter as leading inquiry merely into the arctic regions. From those deductions, however, one good consequence results. The current to the southward, which appears to borrow its chief supply from the great Tartarian torrents, which empty themselves into the Icy Ocean, and are there, in consequence of the centrifugal action of the globe, forced to continue their motion, seeking an exit by the three openings which surround the Pole, in its progress, carries along the bergs and broken ice, and either deposits them partially in the creeks and bays, or urges them to seek a passage along with its course. The waters thus cleared afford a free passage for navigation, and as Hearn saw a portion of this very sea clear and navigable, so, I trust, will the persons embarked in the present expedition merit to be congratulated on their return for having traced out the whole of the arctic shores of North America without danger or obstruction.

The north-easterly winds impel the broken ice towards those shores, and will demand the utmost vigilance to guard against such destructive company in case of contrary winds. The prudence and caution of the mariner are in every instance praiseworthy; but, in the present instance, I may be indulged in directing his attention most earnestly to the form and character of the clouds, and such other matters as are contained in my Journal. Previous experience or superior information may render this admonition superfluous; but, even if it be so, I have much satisfaction in being able to communicate so much as I have done. However, assuming to myself the credit of faithfully representing those facts which have come directly under my observation, it is very remote from my expectation, that my communications will not be considered of value, both from the accuracy of detail and the intention with which they are advanced.

As no doubt of the final success of the expedition rests upon my mind, we shall follow up the inquiry, by way of anticipation on the course to be pursued. Passing by the channels through which the southern current makes its progress into Hudson's Bay through Chesterfield's Inlet or Repulse Bay, and also crossing over the entrance of the great bay observed by Hearn, a tract of coast presents itself totally unknown, and upon whose border the most prominent difficulties stand. The narrow outlet for the ice by Behring's Strait is the chief cause of those difficulties; because, if the polar accumulation extend so far to the westward as to come in contact with the American coast, all further inquiry will be fruitless. If, however, the icy continent extend not so far, as I have much ground to imagine, from Hearn's seeing open water, the voyage will proceed prosperously, and the long desired end will be triumphantly attained. The whole, if actively investigated, will be effected within the space of one month after departing from the latitude of Disko; but the greatest precaution should be observed in noting the different state of the ice on the progress westward; otherwise a return may be attended with disappointment and danger, in the present infant state of the design; particularly if the north-east winds have driven the ice towards the shores of Cumberland Isle. At future periods experience will point out the actual situation of the ice in the latter season, of which a regular record should be deposited in the care of the Royal Society, as it may hereafter be found of the greatest benefit when those seas become frequented by trading vessels.

It would not at the first attempt be adviseable to search the coasts to the southward, with intent to find a passage towards Cook's River, the northern termination of which is still unknown. The expedition directed immediately to the westward towards Behring's Strait may more effectually accomplish its objects, and will probably have to compliment the Russian expedition, under Kotzebue, long before it will have doubled the Prince of Wales's Cape.

What a prospect lies before the mind after the British expedition has passed Behring's Strait! The vast expanse of the northern Pacific spread boundless to the view, with a surface almost trackless, containing numerous islands not hitherto discovered, whose inhabitants will receive the advantages of European commerce, and British constitutional laws! The produce of those islands will hereafter amply reward the trouble of research, discoveries new to science and of value to more civilized society being unfolded, the history of the earth, and a knowledge of its population more accurately determined, and the general state of human kind ameliorated!

Islands as yet undiscovered are not classed alone as likely to participate in those advantages. The extensive and populous empires of Japan and China, beset by the true principles of civilization from the eastern and western intercourse with Europeans, will by degrees learn to lay aside their barbarous caution, and blend themselves, in the virtues, sciences, and refinements of society, with the great family of mankind.

The Russian empire in the east will have a new interest to cultivate in the friendship of Great Britain. The Aleutean, or Black Foxes' Islands, are the right of England in consequence of Cook's discovery; and Bristol Bay, to the north-east of them, may be hereafter an emporium for the Japanese, Chinese, Russian, and British trade, which will turn infinitely to the advantage of the latter.

The Japanese differ in person little from the Uskeemès, seeming to spring like most other Tartar nations from a common origin. The sea is also the favourite resort of the Japanese in the same manner as of the Uskees. The former, however, by inhabiting more genial climates, where nature presented comforts in greater abundance, have risen to higher refinement, and have a regulated society bound by a code of laws peculiar to themselves, and which are most rigidly enforced. Yet after this indication of advancement, Europeans will still find the manners of the Japanese repulsive, and, though polite, tarnished still with barbarous shades. Their commerce with the Dutch in former times, who treated all other Europeans with jealous and treacherous enmity in order to aggrandize themselves, could not fail to impress most unfavourable notions on semi-barbarians, witnessing such conduct among strangers. With such impressions British commerce will have to contend. The same may be said of the Chinese, who are more cautious and proud, if possible, than the Japanese. Care and circumspection, and respect for their national laws and customs, may reconcile them to European manners again, and recover their confidence.

A fort erected on the promontory of Alaska, or on Queen Charlotte's Island on the North American coast, would be a protection from injury or a safe retreat in case of vessels receiving damage at sea, or other injury or danger. The whole of that immense coast, from Cook's River to New Albion and California, is the property of Great Britain by right of discovery: and it claims particular regard, on account of the invaluable resources with which, as a country unexplored, it may be supposed to abound. That great tract of coast lies mostly in temperate latitudes, and for that reason may suit colonization; and the superabundant population of Europe may be there induced to form new settlements under the protection of the British Government.

Trade with the Mexican and South American States also offers the grandest inducements. The inhabitants of those countries, roused into action from their lethargy of centuries' duration, will soon afford to the speculation of the British merchant such advantages as will lead to a trade so immediate and prompt as must follow the discovery of the north-west passage.

A consideration of the utmost importance also follows that event: a ready and direct communication will thus take place between Britain and her south-eastern colonies. New Holland, and all the islands under British dominion, will then be brought, as it were, in contact with the mother country, and the communications between all kept up with the greatest facility, economy and improvement. It is needless to point out the numerous particular advantages that must accrue to the interests of England, and the future great and immeasurable benefits that must arise to society in general, from an enlarged and multiplied intercourse with the East, by means of the present course by the Capes of Good Hope and Horn, and also by the new course to be discovered.

The importance of this subject viewed in all its great consequences demands the utmost deliberation and also liberal provision for the persons engaged in the expedition. It may therefore appear trivial, and probably be received as an unnecessary hint, that, independently of the comforts of warm clothing, double or even greater stock of provisions, and such other indispensable articles as experience or prudence may suggest, a supply of oil of turpentine should be given to each vessel, as the application of that liquid to any part of the body in a frozen state, will prevent inflammation and its miserable consequences. Parties going ashore, on the investigation of natural objects, or making astronomical observations, should be provided with a quantity of the same material, and they will recollect this advice with satisfaction; and, this object in view, I have little doubt of being excused for intruding a gratuitous opinion.

CONCLUDING OBSERVATIONS.

I SHALL close this volume, with the reader's indulgence, by a rapid sketch of the return of the Thomas to Hull.

On the 24th of July, we started with a fresh breeze at N., when eighteen ships were in sight all proceeding to the southward. Then, for the first time since entering the strait, a rainbow appeared: such a phenomenon is very rarely seen in those latitudes, and its indication has not been ascertained.

The current was now running to the southward about two miles or one mile and a half per hour: at other times, if a strong wind blow, it is known to run nearly five miles an hour: a heavy yellowish white fog bank lay along the land: this was about 72° N.

For several days the wind continued N. E., which was succeeded by a strong breeze at S. by W., which retarded the progress of the ship very much, but which did not last long; a cirrus radiation occurred, the shafts of which were suddenly converted into cirrocumulus.

In latitude 62° 40′ N., the Cape Hen (procellaria gravis) appeared: the ship was nearly in the same latitude on the 23d of the preceding April.

On the 4th of August the wind became a steady breeze at N. E.: latitude at noon by observation 60° 33′ N.

About the midnight of August the 6th, much lightning was observed to issue from behind some heavy fog which loaded the horizon to the southward, and to this succeeded a brilliant display of polar coruscation beginning in the south-east, and traversing the southern region to the north-west. The wind about two hours afterwards shifted to the southward, and continued increasing until evening, when it blew a hard gale with heavy rain. On this day, being in about the latitude of Cape Farewell, the ship's log was again resumed, which duty is suspended whilst the whale ships remain in Davis's Strait, and is only observed in crossing the ocean.

Nothing of much importance during the voyage home. Contrary winds, and frequent calms, made it very tedious, as St. Kilda's came in sight not sooner than the 26th of August, and it was joyfully hailed by the ship's crew.

On the 5th of September, being kept in sight of land beating about in an easterly wind till that date, the ship anchored in Stromness, whence, after a short stay in order to land the Orkney sailors, she sailed for Hull, and on the thirteenth of the same month, came to anchor in the Humber within the Spurn Lights.

THE END.

Zeitfracht Medien GmbH
Ferdinand-Jühlke-Straße 7
99095 Erfurt, Deutschland
produktsicherheit@kolibri360.de